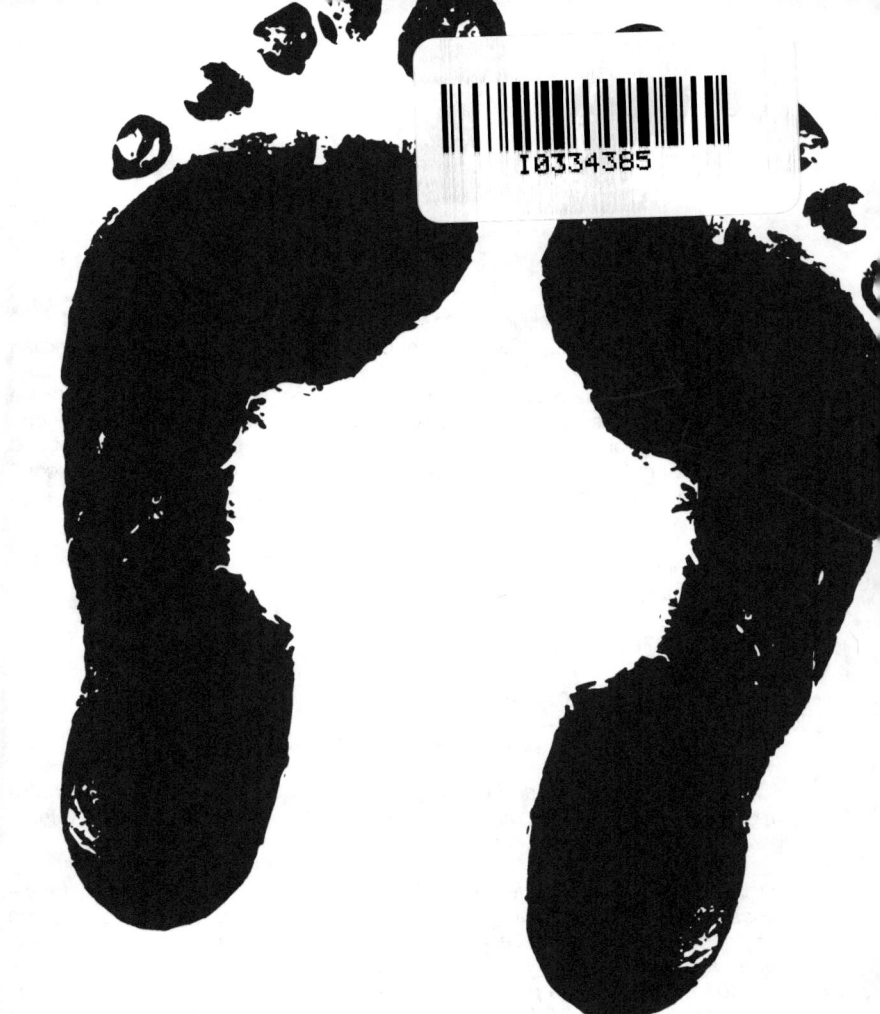

Decisions

Twelve Steps to Land You on God's Pathway

Al Weir, MD

The Christian Medical & Dental Associations was founded in 1931 and currently serves more than 19,000 members; coordinates a network of Christian healthcare professionals for personal and professional growth; sponsors student ministries in medical and dental schools; conducts overseas healthcare projects for underserved populations; addresses policies on healthcare, medical ethics and bioethical and human rights issues; distributes educational and inspirational resources; provides missionary healthcare professionals with continuing education resources; and conducts international academic exchange programs.

For more information:
Christian Medical & Dental Associations
P.O. Box 7500
Bristol, TN 37621-7500
888-230-2637
www.cmda.org • main@cmda.org

Cover design, interior layout and editing by Mandi Mooney.

©2019 by Al Weir, MD, and Christian Medical & Dental Associations. All rights reserved. No part of this publication may be reproduced in any form without written permission from Christian Medical & Dental Associations.

Undesignated Scripture references are taken from the Holy Bible, New International Version®, Copyright ©1973, 1978, 1984, Biblica. Used by permission of Zondervan. All rights reserved. Scripture references marked (ESV) are taken from The ESV® Bible (The Holy Bible, English Standard Version®) copyright ©2001 by Crossway, a publishing ministry of Good News Publishers. All rights reserved. ESV® Text Edition: 2011. Scripture references marked (NKJV) are taken from the New King James Version®. Copyright ©1982 by Thomas Nelson. Used by permission. All rights reserved.

ISBN 978-0-9897598-9-2

2019939248

Printed in the United States of America

To my wife Becky who, with the Lord's wisdom,
has helped guide me through every major decision of my life.

Table of Contents

Introduction 7

Step One: Wanting God's Will 19

Step Two: Choose Your Target 29

Step Three: Gather the Facts 39

Step Four: Follow His Word 53

Step Five: Seek Wise Counsel 65

Step Six: Respect Your Passions 75

Step Seven: The Centrality of Abiding 83

Step Eight: Listen Hard 93

Step Nine: Obedience 107

Step Ten: Trust 117

Step Eleven: Remove the Sin that Binds and Blinds 141

Step Twelve: Surrender 151

Critical Caveats 161

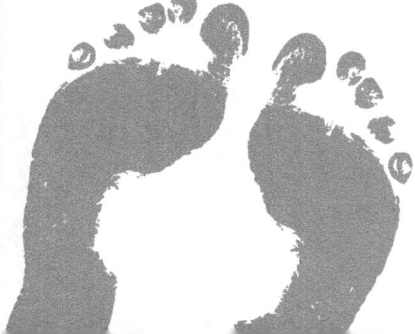

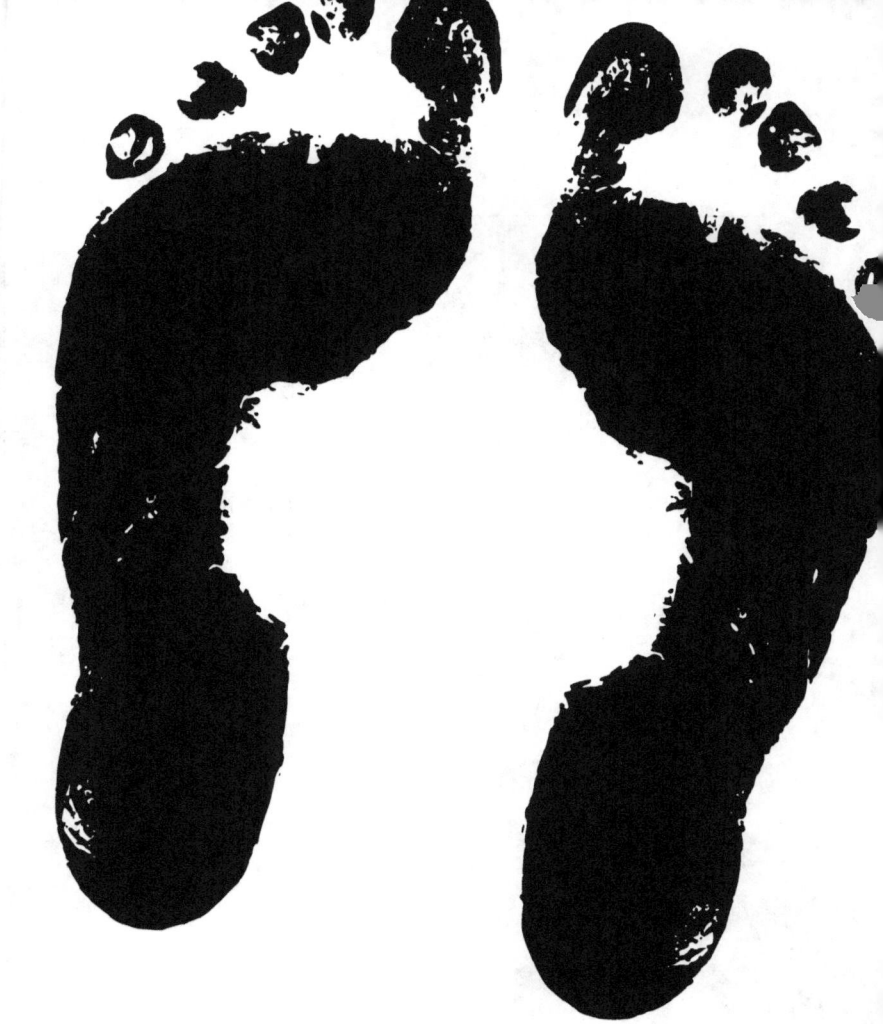

Introduction

> *"In those days Israel had no king; everyone did as he saw fit."*
>
> —Judges 21:25
>
> ---
>
> *"True religion is betting your life that there is a God."*
>
> —Donald Hankey

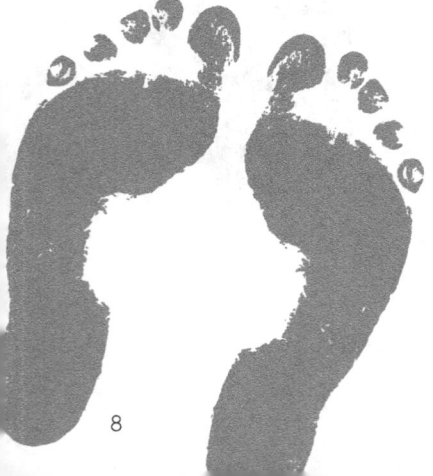

Introduction

Many of us still bow our heads when we hear the story.

Todd Beamer, an ordinary Christian like most of us, was raised in a Christian home and finished college at Wheaton, where he met Lisa, his future bride. He originally looked forward toward a career in medicine but decided on business, became captain of the basketball team and eventually took a job selling systems applications and database software. He was a Sunday School teacher and the father of two, with one more on the way—a normal Christian guy.

Shortly after 8 a.m. on September 11, 2001, he boarded United Flight 93 for just another business trip, hoping to be home the next day. As most of us remember, the plane was flying over Eastern Ohio when terrorists slit the throats of the pilot and co-pilot, took over the plane and turned it toward Washington, D.C. A half hour before, two other flights had flown into the Twin Towers of the World Trade Center while one more crashed into the Pentagon, killing thousands.

Cell phone conversations from passengers during the flight tell the story. Flight 93 passengers were aware of the other hijacked flights and the tragedy they had caused. Todd Beamer and others gathered in conversation and decided to take the plane back. As they prepared to act, Beamer recited the Lord's Prayer and the 23rd Psalm. The last words heard by Beamer over the in-flight telephone were, "Are you guys ready? Okay. Let's roll."

We are a decision-making people. But how do we get there? How did the heroes of Flight 93 make the decision to sacrifice themselves in order to save so many more? As humans created by God, we are not fashioned as robots or puppets to be jerked around by some unseen puppeteer. We are fashioned in love with the freedom and responsibility to choose how we might live.

Many of us, like Todd Beamer, are *Christian* decision-making people.

We who have chosen that path of truth in Christ do not lose the freedom to decide which way we will turn or which direction we will walk. At the same time, we are committed to the One who is willing to show us the way.

How do we make our personal choices while we are seeking to follow the Christ who walks before us? Most of our choices are not as life altering as those on Flight 93, but they are important, not only for us in the moment, but also to God's kingdom plan overall. How do we get it right when we choose our mate, choose our job and choose between business opportunities, relationship possibilities, ministry options or medical therapies?

Certainly, we must seek to fit our lives into the context of God's great redemptive story. We are all part of God's big story and want to fit well within it for His glory. We know God has an important place in His plan for each of us within that story: a task, a location, a life that moves His great plan of redemption through history. Thank God He is willing to let us be part of that plan. Sometimes we struggle mightily to discover what our part will be. Perhaps this mighty struggle, over which I have spent so much time and energy pursuing, is a wasted effort. Perhaps we just need to rest in the will of God. Perhaps God will place us within His perfect plan for our lives if we but do the things He has already made clear to us. There exist at least five clear mandates that define the life of a Christian. If we adhere to these, perhaps our part in His plan will flow naturally from that compliance and we won't have to struggle finding His will. It is abundantly clear God wants us to:

1. Love: both Him and man.

2. Glorify Him: through worship and witness.

3. Seek Him: Him first and then His will.

4. Obey Him: the best we can, through His power, with the light He has given us.

5. Trust Him: He knows, He cares, He can.

If we love, seek, obey, trust and glorify our God, we may not always clearly see that we are in God's great plan for our lives, but I suspect we will nearly always be in that plan and our lives will accomplish the purpose for which we have been created. There is precious freedom in a life so lived.

Settling into God's big story, trusting Him to lay it out, is possibly all we need to do. But we are human and, as such, are focused during most of our lives on our own little stories filled with countless opportunities and countless relationships, all of which require short-term decision-making. I suspect these day-to-day decision-making opportunities are provided as part of God's plan, not only that we might accomplish His will in history, but also that He might make us into the people He wants us to be. So how do we make these sometimes pleasant but often gut-wrenching day-to-day decisions? How do we make them in a way that best places us within God's great redemptive story?

I love Robert Frost's poem "The Road Not Taken," which he introduces with the lines,

"Two roads diverged in a yellow wood,
And sorry I could not travel both
And be one traveler, long I stood
And looked down one as far as I could.
To where it bent in the undergrowth..."

The truth is, we cannot travel both roads when we come to important decisions. We must choose. How does a follower of Christ go about making those choices in faith, making decisions that are pleasing to God?

In my experience, both personally and in observing others, devoted followers of Christ live their decision-making lives in two ways.

The first is more common.

1. My Path

Most of us live life according to our common sense, based on goals we have chosen for ourselves while we are trying to stay within biblical boundaries. This is basically a "My Path, with God on the side" lifestyle where we ask God to hit us if He needs us. We pretty much map out our direction and make choices by examining the data at the time, choosing pathways based on our life goals.

This common sense, "My Path," often leads to Yogi Berra-type guidance from the world around us, such as: "When you come to a fork in the road, take it." Or "We're lost but we're making good time." As a consequence, we tend to move by emotion or inertia without a solid decision-making foundation.

2. Deliberately Seeking

The second way Christ followers might choose to make decisions is with a "Deliberately Seeking" lifestyle where we ask God to choose our life goals and define for us the path to reach those goals. This is a life of "mission, not me," a life that believes we are created with a purpose far greater than ourselves, a purpose that might not meet our personal chosen life goals but should meet His chosen goals for our lives, goals with eternal consequences in God's great plan to redeem this world.

So, the first choice in laying the foundation for decision-making as Christians is this choice: "My Path, with God on the Side" or "Deliberately Seeking." Which choice are we committed to making?

Say we get that choice right and we do choose a life deliberately seeking God's will. Unfortunately, because of who we are, we often run into another problem, a problem of hearing. And this one really frustrates us. "Why won't you speak clearly to me, God?"

I hear this question every week from some Christian friend, and then I quote it once a month myself. Why does God make it so difficult to hear Him speak even when we really want to do so?

In my own life, there are at least three reasons I may not hear God speak when I seek guidance.

1. God's Choice

First of all, God may not be ready to speak yet. He may be doing something of value in the world or in our lives that demands His silence and our patience. Not because He is too busy, but because His plans are so intricate and so profound that timing may be critical. His silence demands my patience to allow Him to work things out in His way.

2. Noise

Secondly, we may not hear Him because the world we have chosen to inhabit produces too much noise to hear His whisper. God often speaks in whispers, perhaps because He wants us to lean in hard to hear Him.

When Elijah had the prophets of Baal slaughtered, Jezebel was displeased and Elijah ran. "Elijah was afraid and ran for his life" (1 Kings 19:3). One night hiding in a cave, Elijah heard the Lord challenge his fear, "What are you doing here, Elijah?" (1 Kings 19:9b). When Elijah had voiced his fear, "The Lord said, 'Go out and stand on the mountain in the presence of the Lord, for the Lord is about to pass by.' Then a great and powerful wind tore the mountains apart and shattered the rocks before the Lord, but the Lord was not in the wind. After the wind there was an earthquake, but the Lord was not in the earthquake. After the earthquake came a fire, but the Lord was not in the fire. And after the fire came a gentle whisper. When Elijah heard it, he pulled his cloak over his face and went out and stood at the mouth of the cave" (1 Kings 19:11-13).

If God chose to whisper to Elijah, who am I to demand a megaphone?

God often walks in shadows and speaks in whispers. If we have built a loud and busy world around ourselves, we may miss those whispers and fail to see Him in the shadows. How noisy is your world? Some Christians are faithful enough to hear God speak in hectic, chaotic, noisy places, but most of us require more peace and quiet to listen for God's direction. We have to create that quiet in one of two ways.

First, we can deliberately set aside times and places where the world can't creep in to find us, like our kitchen table before the sun rises or the back porch at night. We can take these special times of quiet focus and seek His voice away from the noisy marketplace. How many of us do this regularly?

Arnie was retired from his orthopedic practice and helping lead a retreat for Christian healthcare professionals. He did not know he would be the one who was changed. Based on Dallas Willard's book Hearing God, *the retreat speaker challenged his audience, "I want you each to take the next five minutes and just listen to the Lord in silence." Arnie took up the challenge. After three minutes of silent listening, Arnie heard God ask him in the silence, "How are you spending your time?" From that moment, Arnie's life was rearranged. A great deal of time previously spent on stock market analysis and sports television viewing was transformed into time of service for the King.*

Sometimes we just need to stop and create quiet so God's whisper can be heard.

Additionally, we can simplify our lifestyles, make changes in the way we do life that de-clutter our lives and remove the noise that comes with too many unimportant responsibilities and too many unnecessary pleasures. What do I need to remove from my life to reduce the noise and allow God's whisper to get through? Make a list of even one thing and

God may finally get His message through.

3. Deliberate Deafness

Our deafness to God's whisper may be His choice or our noise, or, finally, we may miss His voice due to deliberate deafness.

A couple of years ago, my daughter Catherine and her husband Lance took their two daughters and newborn son to Disney World. After a hot day standing in lines and carrying little children too tired to walk themselves, they returned to the hotel to get ready for dinner. Elaina was five and Lyla was three. As Mom and Dad were dealing with their newborn son, they told the girls to go get ready for their bath. After a couple of minutes, Elaina came to the bedroom and said, "Lyla locked the door."

"What do you mean, Lyla locked the door?"

"She went in the bathroom and won't let me in."

Catherine went to the door and knocked, "Lyla, can you open the door?"

The only sound in reply was running bathtub water.

"Lyla, open the door!"

Now Mom was scared: her 3-year-old precious daughter in a locked bathroom, running water, silence, visions of tragedy on the far side of the door.

"Lance!"

Lance banged on the door, "Lyla! Open this door!"

No sound but running bath water.

In desperation and fear, Lance kicked down the hotel

room door and rushed in to save his daughter. He found her lying face up in the tub's water, her eyes wide open with her fingers in her ears, repeating over and over, "I do not want to hear you. I do not want to hear you."

Lance grabbed Lyla up in his arms with tears running down his face, hugged her, then spanked her, then hugged her again. He then handed her to her mother and went to pay for the broken door.

Sometimes God speaks quite loudly enough for the ambient noise, but we stubbornly plug our ears, "I do not want to hear you. I do not want to hear you."

This refusal to listen may come because God's voice is calling us to change. Almost always the voice of God comes for one of two reasons: so we may be comforted or so we may be changed. We may be caught in a relationship He wants us to leave, or we may be caught in a pleasure that is wasting His time, or we may be caught in a mission that is ours and not His. Whatever the reasons that have placed the fingers in our ears, we will not hear His guidance until we remove them and change according to His direction. This loss of hearing is a matter of the will.

And so, if we want to hear our Lord, we must come seeking His direction: with the foundation of our life as mission, with the noise of our world dampened to the best of our ability and with our ears wide open, ready to hear, ready to change, ready to make the choice God would have us make for His glory and the redemption of the world.

But what if I do all of this and still don't know which job I should take, whom to marry or which medical therapy I should choose?

What next?

Looking back over a life of guiding other Christians through countless decisions, and struggling with my own, I would like to take you down twelve steps on the pathway to God's will. Each step has value in itself. Some steps are absolutely essential. Together they will land you on God's path, guaranteed by God's Word, whatever the decision before you.

Explore these steps. Follow them with specific decisions in mind. Pray through them as you examine your life. If you follow them fully, you will end up on His path, guaranteed.

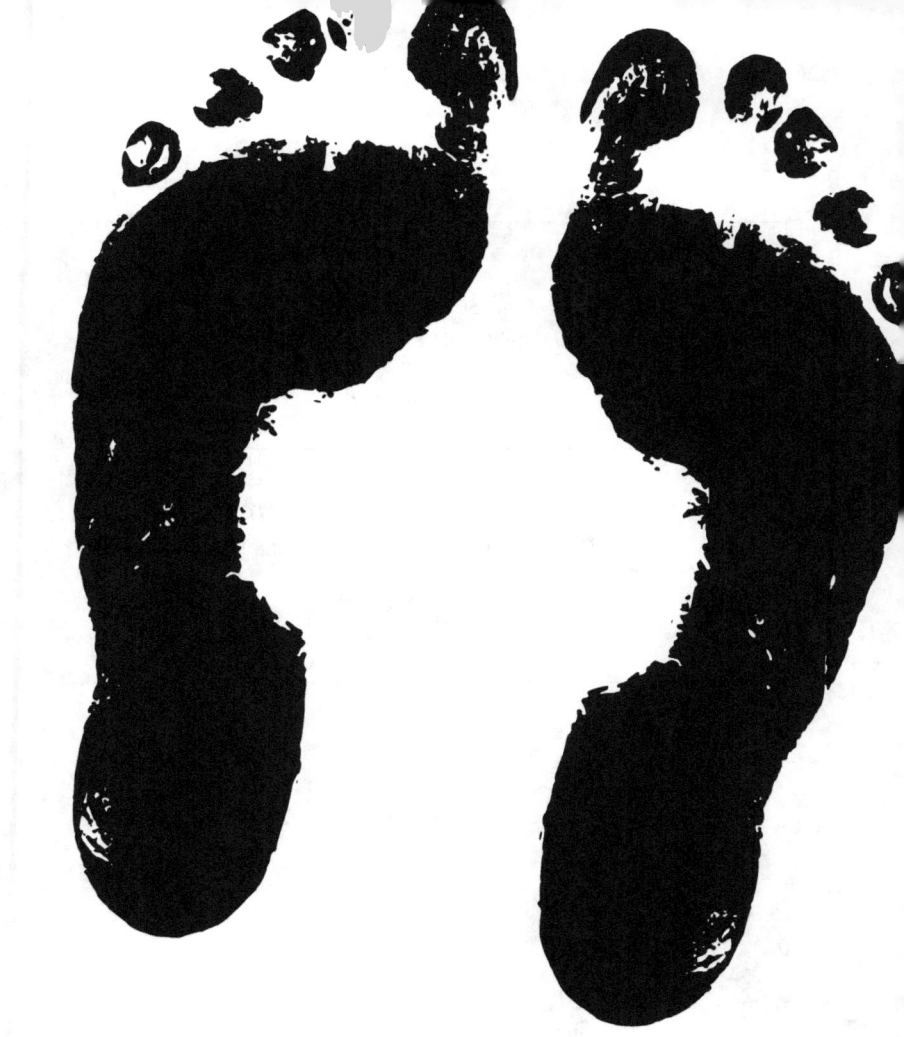

Step One
Wanting God's Will

> *"You will seek me and find me
> when you seek me with all your heart."*
>
> —Jeremiah 29:13
>
> ---
>
> *"Give to me, take away from me,
> but make my will conform to yours."*
>
> —Paschal

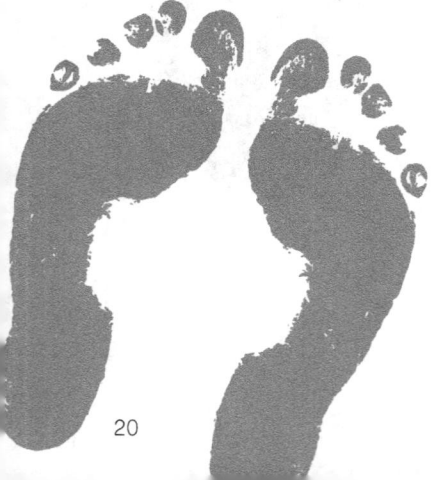

Step One
Wanting God's Will

It is a non-vital decision. No one's life or health is dependent on it. God's kingdom will continue whichever path is chosen—but a decision must be made.

Over the years of building our lives we had bought a small lake house, like the one my folks leased when I was a teenager with all those grand memories of skiing, fishing and holding hands at sunset with my future bride. We really bought the place for our kids and their kids to enjoy—and they did. Now God has been calling us into a simplified life, calling us into continued service in new ways. Do we sell this lake house as part of God's plan? Our daughter begs for us to keep it for her small children and for her memories of her own lakeside adventures with friends growing up. The peacefulness of the place is awesome, the escape from a fast-paced practice of medicine, the lack of time pressure, the beauty of God riding on the wings of the egret that fishes from our pier, the many retreats for Christian youth who still expect to come there in the years to come—all good, all blessed by God. We love the place. And yet, we have a clear understanding that God wishes us to simplify dramatically our lifestyle, for Him, for His glory, for His plan in redeeming the world. How do we decide?

I choose this illustration specifically because it is an everyday decision, not a give-my-life-to-missions decision. God puts the eternal into our everyday decisions, and it is here we must most often find our way into His will.

It has become clear to me over the years that the greatest impediment for me in finding God's will is the desire of my heart. I am least able to let go of that which God would have me release when my heart is wrapped around it. I am least able to persevere in some difficult place where God would have me remain if my heart is begging to leave. My personal desires lie as fallen trees across the paths where God would have me travel, obstructing my way, or they lead me like the distant sound of beautiful music down paths He would have me avoid.

It is these personal desires that most often prevent me from making God's best decision in my life. They plug my ears and blind my eyes to His message. And thus, I believe that *99 percent of finding God's will is wanting God's will.*

I am totally convinced that my chief task in Christian decision-making is to want God's will with all my heart. It is then God's task to show it to me. This doesn't necessarily mean that, just because I want very much to keep the lake house, it must be outside of God's will. But it does mean I might miss His will in this decision completely if I do not lay that desire as a sacrifice at His feet.

For some reason God wants our will as much as He wants anything in our lives. He wants us to trust Him to be our good Father, our King. He wants us to acknowledge that His ways are better than ours, for His ways are rooted in love and pointed toward the redemption of His creation.

Specifically, in the issue of finding His will, He tells us through Jeremiah, "You will seek me and find me when you seek me with *all your heart*" (Jeremiah 29:13). And again He reminds us through Solomon, "Trust in the Lord with *all your heart* and lean not on your own understanding; in all your ways acknowledge him, and he will make your paths straight" (Proverbs 3:5-6).

God longs for our hearts more than anything else we can offer, much like I long for my children to love me, far more than anything else they could give me. And if we long for Him, He will show us the way to most please Him, the direction He would most want us to travel. It is my business is to seek God's will, rather than my own, with all my heart; it is His business to show me the way.

This brings us to a central understanding about our role in life. Is life about *me*?

I have an extremely hard time not making life about me. Each of us has a central pivot in our lives that can turn us one way or another. Depending on how we choose to turn, life is either *mission* or *me*. Either my central focus in life is living for God and those He loves, or my central focus in life is living for me and those I love. They are in no way exclusive, but the direction we choose will make all the difference in finding God's will for our decision-making. As Robert Frost reminded us, "Two roads diverged in a yellow wood." The farther we travel down one, the harder it is to find the other. One path is *my way*, the other is *His way*. We must choose.

Conditions

Choosing to want God's will is not always easy or straightforward. I often want His will but then decide to place conditions on that desire. I'm not alone in struggling with this; others have figured it out better than I.

> *Rusty and I grew up together. I knew him when comfort was a significant requirement for life. But then he and his wife Carol changed directions to serve God in a dangerous and uncomfortable part of the world. "People ask us how we decided to work in Afghanistan. It's simple. We just took away all the conditions we had placed on God as a requirement for service—'not there, with this security, this financial package, this side of the ocean, this language, this long, etc.' When we removed all of our conditions and just asked God to use us how He wanted, we ended up where we are, and we are happy to be there."*

Rusty and his wife settled into a life where their joy was not controlled by circumstances. That which had been important to satisfy their lives was no longer important. Their lives were no longer "about me." How many of us wish we could face each day with satisfaction, regardless of the threats to the life we had planned? Rusty found the key—it was not by gaining more control over his life, but it was by letting go of the reins and handing them over to God. It was by removing all the conditions he had set before God and saying, "Whatever it takes, God, place me in your will."

So, what conditions have I set before the Lord? "We can go this far ... but no farther." What blessings, what achievements does God have waiting for me beyond the boundaries of my conditions?

Tom Blumer was a friend of mine who died recently from cancer. He was a true man of God. When he began his cancer journey, after his first surgery, Tom told me, "The surgeon is not sure he can get it all, but, hey man, for me it's a win, win situation. Whatever God wants—just like when my son Eric got leukemia. When Eric got leukemia, I prayed, 'God, this is my son; you know how I feel. You know how much I love him and what I want. But you gave him to me and I thank you for that. I now give him to you. Please save him, but your will be done.'" Eric was saved. Now, many years later, Tom faced his own health crisis. Throughout Tom's illness—the discovery of his cancer, the initial surgeries and chemotherapy, the recurrence, advanced surgery and treatment, the word he was going to die from his illness—he was a man of faith. His faith was not the weak kind that says, "I have faith that God is going to heal me," but the strongest kind of faith that said, "I want badly to live, to be with my family, but whatever you want, Lord, it's okay with me."

Does my trust in my God allow me to want His will even when it might bring me harm?

Job once cried out, "Though He slay me, yet will I trust him" (Job 13:15a, NKJV). How much do I really want God's will?

Vacillations

One of my frustrations in wanting God's will is that I want His will during my morning devotions and then lose that desire as the day works out in my life.

I remember clearly one weekend morning when, on a day off, I ran into the hospital to see a friend who had been admitted for atrial fibrillation. While there, I took some additional time to catch up on some chart work to make the next week easier. But I still had control of the rest of my day. As I was finishing at the computer, a friend for whom I pray regularly called and wanted to meet me for coffee and concerns. I accepted but was frustrated because I had just finished squeezing the margin out of my weekend with the hospital visit and chart work. Now I would be time-pressured for the rest of my day off.

And then God spoke clearly to me, "Didn't you ask me this morning to empty you so that I might fill you, so that the broken might be made whole again? Was that you praying this morning? Isn't this man broken?"

How can I be so sincere in my prayer life at morning devotions and then totally out of spirit when God actually presents me with an opportunity to follow His will? Why was I not thrilled for God to use me in the life of this man for whom I was praying? From where comes this disconnect between my very deep beliefs, my very sincere prayers and my daily living? Why don't I live what I desperately believe? Do I really want His will in my life if I can vacillate so freely in my desire to follow it?

It's not like I am unaware of my contradictory behavior. I've lived too long to be surprised by my inconsistencies—but I am quite perturbed and saddened by them.

This is not what I want for my life. How do I change so my desire to follow God's will in the morning sticks with me throughout my day? I honestly don't know.

I know of little I can do to authenticate my life other than to seek Him sincerely, surrender my disconnected life to be filled by Him regularly, worship in community, obey when I hear Him speak and trust He can work out His best within my inconsistencies and vacillations. I'm betting my life He can.

Letting Go

Oswald Chambers made it clear, "The essence of sin is my claim to my right to myself." Do I claim the right to make my own decisions in life? Do I make my decisions choosing my desires rather than His, my will rather than His? The 17th century priest and devotional writer François Fenelon once wrote, "All that lies within your power is the direction of your will." Which direction will I choose to point my will in this heart-filled decision about a house on the lake? Which direction will you choose to point your will in your heart-filled decision about your job, your future spouse, your ministry, your money, your suffering, your child, your pleasure?

Blaise Pascal was a 17th century physician, mathematician and lover of Christ who wrote: "I do not ask for health or sickness or life or death: I ask that you dispose of my health and sickness, my life and death—for your glory, for my salvation, for the use of your church and the saints of which I am a part...Give to me; take away from me; but make my will conform to yours."

In this frame of mind, in this state of heart, we are most likely to make decisions that follow God's best plan for our lives.

But what if we are not there yet? What if we don't really want God's will more than our own, particularly in a given area where a decision needs to be made? I love my mom, now 92 years old, who is always honest about her faith. Sometimes when facing a difficult circumstance in life she would say, "I don't want to do God's will in this, but I want to want to." That's where I sometimes find myself. I don't really feel totally committed to doing God's will in a given decision, but "I want to want to."

If this is where we are, then this is the truth of life, and God will work with us. How do we get from wanting to want His will to wanting His will with all of our hearts?

Three simple suggestions before we move on:

1. *Spend more time with Jesus.* The more we know Him, the more we love Him; and the more we love Him, the more

we trust Him and understand that His love wants the best for us. Spend more time in prayer. Spend more time in reading His Word. Spend more time recalling Him to your consciousness as you walk through your normal life.

2. *Obey Him in the small things He has shown to you.* When we obey, we see whether or not He is trustworthy, and we see Him act in our lives in beautiful ways.

3. *Spend time in fellowship with others who love our Lord.* The desire to follow Christ is contagious. When we see others who are sold out for Christ, we catch that through His Spirit and the desire to follow His will grows in our hearts.

God is a patient Father. He is constantly drawing us closer. We are constantly being transformed in this life by His Spirit. We need to approach God from where we are, not from where we wish we could be. And that's enough. If we just want to want His will, He will work with us and guide us to place us on the right path.

99 percent of finding God's will is wanting God's will.

Next Steps

Lay out in writing below a decision that needs to be made in all its complexities.

_____
_____
_____
_____
_____
_____
_____
_____
_____
_____

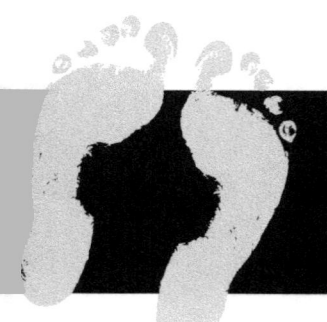

*Dear Father,
I am laying out before you this decision. Whatever direction you choose; I want to follow—not my will but yours be done.
Amen*

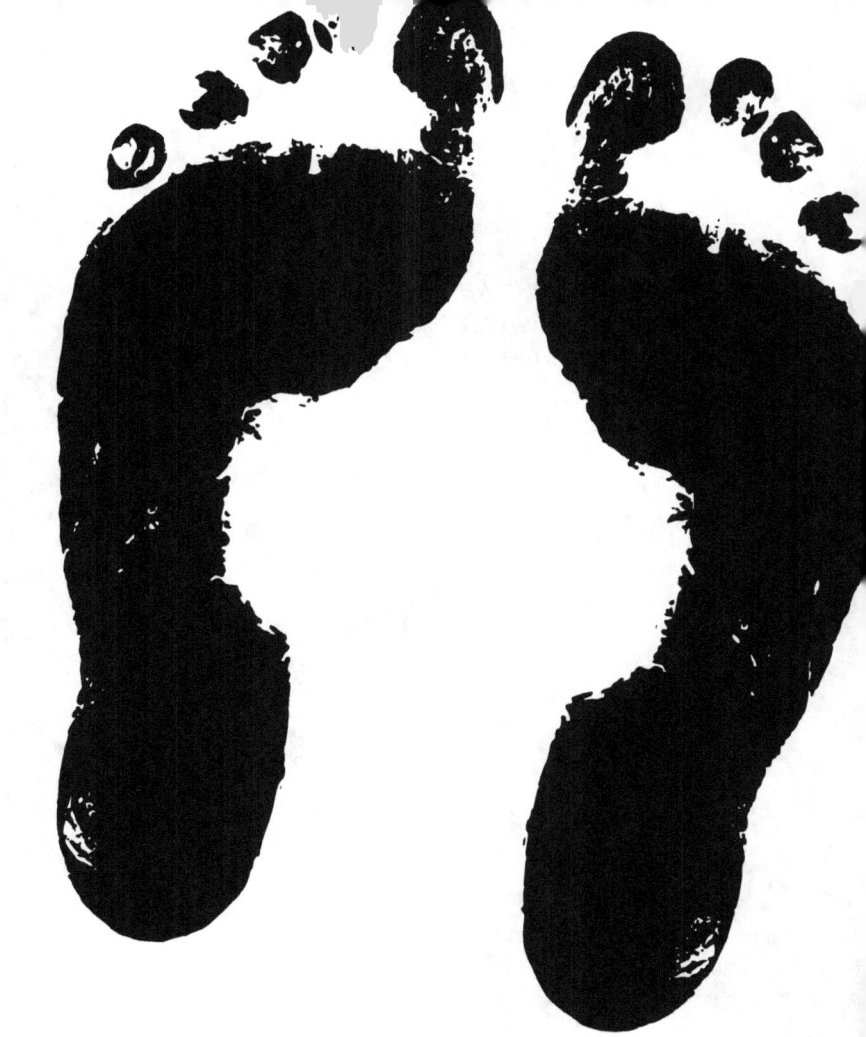

Step Two
Choose Your Target

> "I press on toward the goal to win the prize for which God has called me heavenward in Christ Jesus."
>
> —Philippians 3:14
>
> ---
>
> "If you board the wrong train, it's no use running along the corridor in the opposite direction."
>
> —Dietrich Bonhoeffer

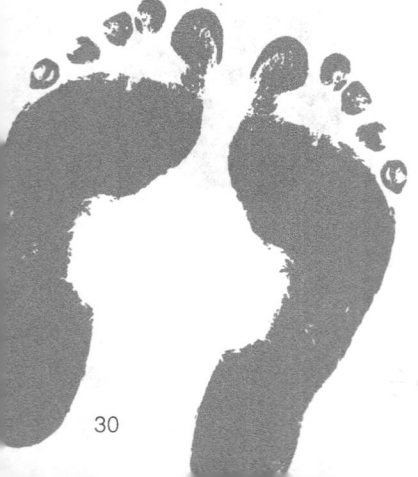

Step Two
Choose Your Target

Ken Jones is a minister and life coach who lives in Northern California. He once gave me some wise advice about directional thinking, "You know, there are two ways to hit a bull's-eye. The conventional way is to draw the bull's-eye, aim your arrow and shoot accurately. The other way is to shoot wherever you choose, find the place the arrow lands and then draw a bull's-eye around it."

When I look at my own life, many of the decisions I settle for are circles drawn around arrows I shot without a clear direction in mind. Life just sort of said, "Shoot there," and I did, and then I did the best I could with the target I hit. Like the time I woke up one day and found I was rich. I had returned from the mission field as a doctor trying to find purpose in life. I found it in caring for cancer patients. I was good at what I did, joined a wonderful group of doctors and worked very hard. I had no target that I was considering for my finances. I just kept working, collecting what was standard and woke up rich one day. I didn't feel guilty about the money, but I felt covered-up, like I was a refrigerator swallowed in magnets, magnets covering me so well no one could see who I really was and how much I loved Jesus. I had hit the bull's-eye of wealth unintentionally because I had not chosen another target. I drew circles around it and made choices based on where I was, rather than where I would have chosen to be, where God would have chosen me to be. When I discovered the target I had drawn, I then had to change my life based on an unintended consequence.

It is vitally important we choose our targets rather than react to the targets the world chooses for us. This is especially true of our ultimate targets. Choosing our ultimate targets early on does a great deal to help us in many temporal decisions along the way.

C.S. Lewis described the value of choosing our ultimate target first, "If we aim at heaven, we get earth thrown in. If we aim at earth, we get neither."

The beauty of choosing our ultimate target first is that this choice allows inertia to work for us in our lifelong decision-making. When an arrow is in flight toward a target, it takes a good deal of energy to have it change direction. Just so, if I am moving in life toward an ultimate target, a decision that might turn me away from that target would require more energy than if I was just hanging out, drifting through life.

For example, if I want as a long-term target to raise a family that honors God, my trajectory toward that target makes it more difficult for me to turn aside to a short-term goal of an intimate relationship with one other than my spouse. If I am committed to my long-term target, that commitment will already have determined the decision about the other relationship and I don't have to consider it.

Or, if I choose as a long-term target to retire from my work at 50 and use the next 20 years to serve in missions, the trajectory toward that target makes it more difficult for me to buy increasingly larger houses and a vacation home in the mountains. My long-term target makes it easier to make the right decision about the property purchases.

Or, take for example my personal target of daily mission, the one I pray for each day during my time of devotion: "Let me rise up and meet You and empty myself for You; fill me, so that the lost may be found in You, the broken made whole in You and that You may be glorified."

It is often in my busy days with patients waiting and the time pressure upon me that I quote this target. If I truly push my energies toward hitting this bull's-eye, the decisions about seeing more patients for higher productivity and greater economic gain have already been made. I can't see patients at maximum speed with minimal time and still develop the relationships needed to accomplish my overarching target, the reason I am caring for them in the first place. Thus, my long-term target has engaged my energy and plotted a trajectory such that my short-term decision-making regarding length of patient visits has been simplified.

A few years ago, my wife and I were having a fairly common type of discussion between spouses. By expanding the breakfast room, we could fit more of the family around the table and enlarge the pantry to provide more storage space. Our discussion hovered around building plans, affordability, interest rates, etc. "Would we rather spend the money on this or on some other project for the house?" Everything fit, and we decided we could go ahead. Then my wife asked the additional question, "Okay, now that we know we can do this, how does it glorify God?"

Sometimes we choose the wrong target in life because we don't ask the right questions. Sometimes we think to ask the small questions, the short-term questions, and fail to ask the big questions that are often directed at long-term goals.

The rich young ruler came to Jesus for direction, "...what must I do to inherit eternal life?" (Luke 18:18). Now that's a long-term, big question. Hopefully, we as Christians get the answer right and know eternal life is all about God's sacrifice and not our merit. But then, once we ask the question and accept the answer, life gets complicated.

Jesus next tells the man to "come, follow me" (Luke 18:22b). Jesus says the same to us, and for the rest of our lives this following demands other big questions in our everyday decision-making. And often we fail to ask them.

As I make decisions in life, I usually rely on reason, common sense and conscience to lead me in the right direction. But, looking back on my life, I realize this approach has not always kept me on God's path. My personal desires are sometimes too strong, even for my Bible-based conscience and my well-educated reason. I am discovering that my bias toward my own interests pushes me forward with impulsive choices, reaching for short-term goals. Instead, I need to stop as I approach major decisions and take a time out, like a surgeon in the operating room or the child who just bit her sister. During this time out I need to ask the big and long-term questions, like the one my wife asked, "How does this glorify God?" and others like, "Will this help me follow Jesus?" and "How does this affect the ultimate long-term goals in my life?"

Asking these questions certainly won't guarantee I will make the right decision; I still may get it wrong because of my self-nature. But at least I bring it up to the King and ask His opinion; at least I attempt to line things up with His ultimate purpose for my life so I am less likely to waste time in pleasant side-trails when God has laid out a glory-road for me to follow.

Many great men have spoken to this necessity of choosing our overall targets wisely.

Dietrich Bonhoeffer was a German pastor and theologian who was hanged for his part in a plot to kill Adolf Hitler, a task he took on as the will of God. Before he was caught up in the war, he trained pastors and, in doing so, noted that so many Christian men and women choose the wrong overarching target for their lives, forcing them to spend tremendous and fruitless energy trying to make their short-term goals compatible with their unfulfilled conscience. He put it this way: "If you board the wrong train, it's no use running along the corridor in the opposite direction."

How frustrating it is to see my life headed in one direction, due to choices I have made, with the face of Christ pressed against the window pane of a train on the tracks just next to me, staring at me with love and sorrow as His train is headed the opposite way.

When we were younger, my father used to warn us, "You can choose your actions, or you can choose your consequences, but you can't choose both." I can either live my life with impulsive decisions and accept the consequences that come, or I can choose my consequences, my targets in life, and let them dictate my actions and my decisions along the way. There are train stations I have chosen never to see when I board the train headed for God's best plan for my life. There are decisions I have chosen never to make if I have made the firm decision to follow Jesus.

Os Guinness grew up in China. When he was five years old, because of the paucity of good schools in Nanjing, he was sent to a boarding school in Shanghai. In his book *Impossible People*, he describes how his parents gave him the right targets to shoot for in his life away from home:

"To give me a constant reminder of the North Star of the faith at the center of our family life, my father had searched for two, small, flat stones and painted on them his life motto and that of my mother. For many years those two little stones were tangible memos in the pockets of my gray flannel shorts that were the uniform of most English schoolboys in those days. In my right-hand pocket was my father's motto, "Found Faithful," and in my left-hand pocket was my mother's, "Please Him."

From such an early age Os Guinness learned the value of having a target to shoot for in his life.

The quote that makes me most concerned about the directional decisions in my own life comes from Dwight L Moody, the great 19th century pastor: "Our greatest fear in life should not be of failure, but of succeeding at things in life that don't really matter."

I fear God might say this of my life someday. Will God view the short-term targets in my life as "things that don't really matter?" Will I be hitting bull's-eyes that don't count? Have I, in my highest moments, chosen the ultimate bull's-eye for my life? Paul chose his target well and Jesus completed the bull's-eye: "I press on toward the goal to win the prize for which God has called me heavenward in Christ Jesus" (Philippians 3:14).

My target for life is to run into the arms of Jesus and hear Him say, "Well done, good and faithful servant." The arrow I shoot with my life is pressing on to win that prize.

And so, am I committed to shooting the arrow of my life in one direction toward my ultimate target? Am I choosing other worthwhile, long-term targets to shoot for as I travel?

Paul gave us some good guidelines: "Finally, brothers, whatever is true, whatever is honorable, whatever is just, whatever is pure, whatever is lovely, whatever is commendable, if there is any excellence, if there is anything worthy of praise, think about these things" (Philippians 4:8, ESV).

We should not only "think about these things," but we should use them as a measuring stick to gauge the value of our targets. We should use them to first choose our long-term targets, and then, as we fly toward the targets-worth-shooting-for, countless short-term decisions will come our way. If we stay true to our chosen trajectories, much of the anxiety of decision-making will zoom by without turning us. Many of life's choices will become obvious because they do or do not follow my flight plan.

Next Steps

List four major long-term targets for your life.

1. _____

2. _____

3. _____

4. _____

Describe how each target might affect the decision you are facing.

1. _____

2. _____

3. _____

4. _____

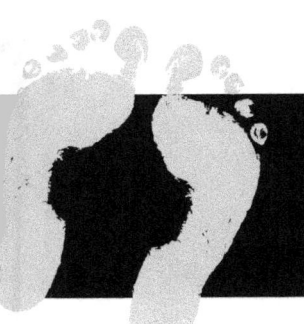

*Dear Father,
Help me define the long-term targets for my life that will most glorify your name. And then let me fly without veering.
Amen*

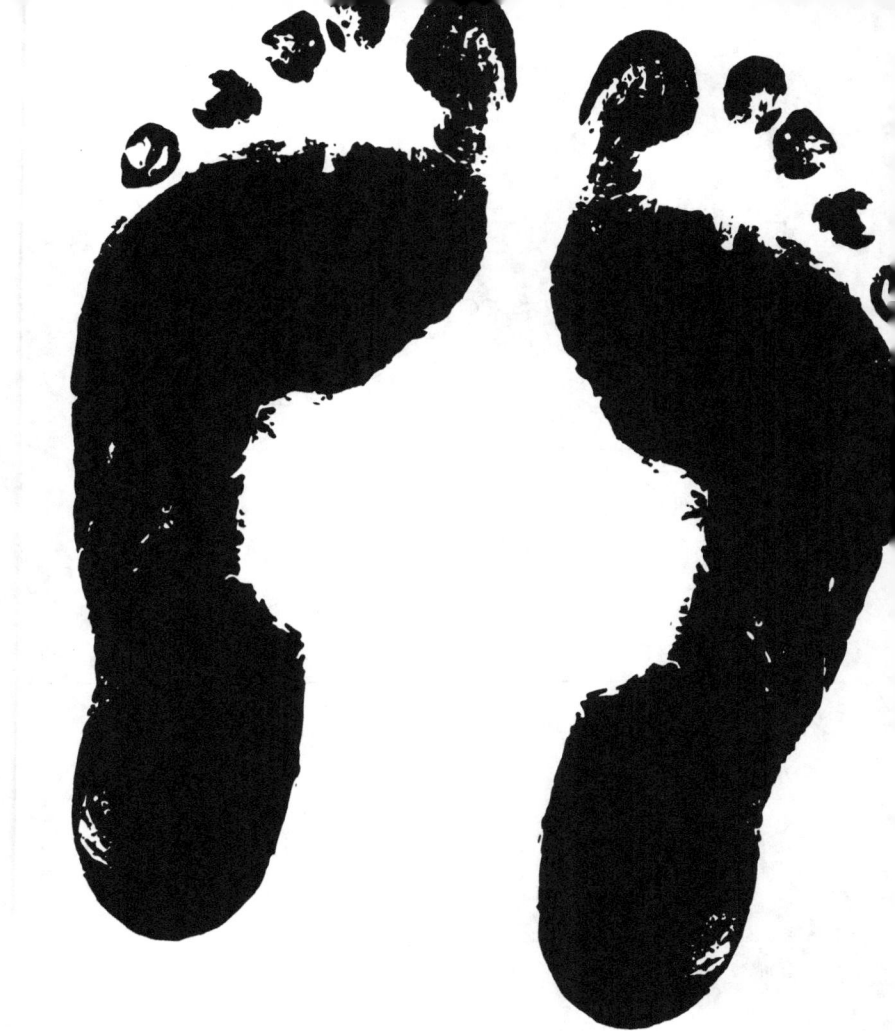

Step Three
Gather the Facts

> "...men of Issachar, who understood the times and knew what Israel should do..."
>
> —1 Chronicles 12:32
>
> ---
>
> "When you reckon things up, bring God in as the greatest factor in your calculations."
>
> —Oswald Chambers

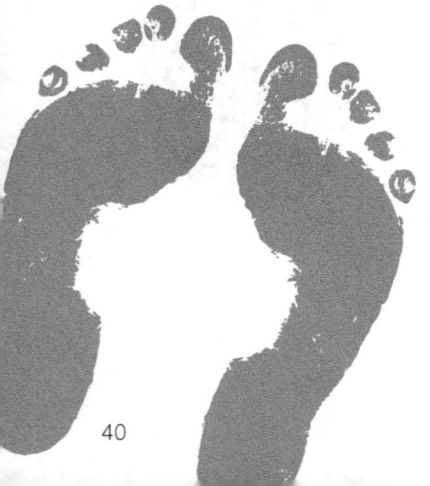

Step Three
Gather the Facts

Jon is a medical student who contacts me periodically for advice. He is a dedicated follower of Christ who plans to spend his life on an international mission field. He is graduating from medical school next year and wants badly to become an orthopedic surgeon. He has the opportunity to spend a few weeks this spring with a missionary surgeon in South America and has been excited about that venture. He contacted me by email for help in a decision he had to make, "I have my Step 1 exams coming up just before the mission trip. I will have to take the Step 1 exam early if I go. Also, my advisor tells me I would have a better chance in getting an orthopedic residency if I stayed in town and spent the time with some local orthopedic doctors. Should I still go on the mission trip?"

My first word of advice was that he should be sure he is seeking God's will rather than his own about the decision. Then I told him I needed more information to help advise. Had he made a commitment to the missionary that he would come? With his overarching, long-term target requiring graduation from medical school, did he have enough time to prepare for the exams to do well? In what ways, specifically, could working with local orthopedic surgeons advance his chances of obtaining a residency position? Besides seeking God's will, he also needed to gather more information in order to make a wise, God-honoring decision.

Impulsive decision-making without adequate information can sometimes back you into God's best plan, but often leads into a maze of wandering before you can find your way back to the right path. I know from experience.

When I left the practice of medicine for a few years to serve the

Lord with Christian Medical & Dental Associations, I committed to let my wife build a house she could love in order to decrease the sacrifice she made in leaving her life as a prominent doctor's wife. That decision was good. What followed would have worked out better had we gathered the facts before moving forward. The plot of land we chose was adjacent to our ministry campus, with a short and beautiful walk through the woods to work each day. It was situated on a hillside, where we decided to build a flatlander's home. Amazing amounts of earth were moved; after which, the carved-out hillside had to be supported by that which came to be known as The Great Wall of Bristol. The expense was overwhelming because we did not gather the facts before we made the decisions in building. I take all the credit for drifting through that process without the information needed to honor God with our decision-making. In doing so, I financially impacted our ability to do many things for the Lord that have followed since then. God has given us minds He wishes us to use in our decision-making, and the only way to do that well is to feed them with the appropriate facts. Impulsive decision-making without taking the time to gather the facts has chained many Christians to a life of necessity rather than a life of grand adventure with the Lord.

Choosing the Questions

How do you go about gathering the facts needed to make a decision? How do we know what questions to ask? Probably the best approach in choosing the proper questions is to check with those who have made similar decisions of their own, as well as those who have helped others through such decision-making.

When patients come to me for advice regarding a new diagnosis of cancer or an upcoming doctor visit, they know they will have to face some difficult decisions. They consistently raise the question, "What should I ask the doctor?" I give them the following list:

1. How confident are you of the diagnosis?

2. What will this illness do to the length and quality of my life?

3. What is the best treatment for my problem?

4. Should I seek a second opinion?

5. Are there research programs in which I should consider taking a part?

6. What about alternative and complementary medicines?

7. If I were your sister, what would you tell me to do?

8. Doctor, do you pray with your patients?

I cannot give them all the answers they need, but I have the experience necessary to help them ask the right questions. I then try to connect them with a patient who has gone through the same illness for additional perspective.

So, if I have questions about a financial decision, I should spend time developing my questions with someone who is a financial expert and with someone who has had to make the same decision. If I am making a decision about international missions, I should spend time with my pastor and spend time with those who have been called to and served in missions. The goal of such meetings is not just to hear experiences but also to formulate the correct questions so that I may lay the facts before God and let Him speak into my life through my mind as He also does through my heart.

We must ask these right questions to gather the practical facts. But, while we are asking our questions, God is asking His questions of us. And, as important as ours are to understand the situations surrounding our decisions, God's questions are far more important. Our motive in gathering facts is to know how we can work it all out, so we can do it well for God and minimize the damage to ourselves. We look at our world and appropriate questions start to fly.

When?

What?

How?

Which?

If....?

These are legitimate questions, but they may become the nails holding our feet to the floor when God calls us forward in ways these questions do not answer.

Our insistence that we understand our future sometimes makes it difficult for us to step into God's future. Sometimes we may be immobilized by our questions to God.

God's questions to us are different. God's questions to us are:

- Will you trust me?
- Will you obey me?

Our questions to God don't matter much until we answer His questions to us:

- Will you trust me, whatever?
- Will you obey me, whatever?

Usually, God's questions are not answered with intellect only. Usually, God's questions require action. Very often, the only way to answer God's question is to take the facts, mix them with the whisper of God we hear and then step into the darkness in the direction we hear Him calling.

The Fact of Community

When I was younger and trying to find God's will for my occupation in life, I bounced around a lot. I recall the day I was working in the lab with a fellow physician, speaking of changing to a more clinical field. I had already spent time in internal medicine practice, plus my years on the mission field. Reflecting on my vacillations in occupation thus far, my mentor Eric Lester asked me a profound question, "You know what the problem is with loose cannons, don't you?" At first, I missed the point as I was only thinking of myself as the cannon. Then he answered the question, "It rolls around and smashes everyone else on the deck."

We are not alone. Our great Western culture has ingrained within us the importance of the individual. We have this deep sense that each of us is responsible for our own successes and failures. We've pulled up hard on our own bootstraps to get us where we are and seek to control our own destinies. In the end we plan to sing with Frank Sinatra, "I did it my way."

So many of us see our faith as an individual decision between "I and Thou." We often make our decisions with the same understanding. I suspect God views our faith and our decisions differently.

I know Christ died for me, but I suspect He cares even more for His church, His bride. I suspect God sees us not as millions of isolated, autonomous believers, but as a community, dedicated to His one purpose, holding up one another in our weaknesses, praising Him with one voice, charging arm-in-arm against the gates of hell. Instead of recognizing the import of the community in my decisions, I often find myself having my own little devotion with God, struggling with my own spiritual failures, seeking His direction as if the consequences of that direction fall on me alone. Not so.

Our actions impact those around us. After Jesus died on the cross, all but one of His disciples died as martyrs for their faith. As he wrote in *Insanity of God*, when Nik Ripken followed God's will to Africa, his son died of an asthma attack that would not have taken his life if Nik had remained in America. If I choose wealth as my goal for life, my children will seek after the same goals. If I choose pride for my own life, my children will be addicted to pride. If I choose sacrificial service as the center of my life, my children are more likely to do the same.

A central fact we must consider as we seek God's will in any decision is that the direction we choose will always have consequences for those around us. This should not bring fear into our decision-making, and this should never trump God's will, but this fact should be weighed carefully with all the other facts that are a part of God's process in guiding us into His will.

Taking Time

It is only with adequate information that we can approach decisions in a way that best discovers God's will. But facts alone are like data alone; they need time and wisdom to be organized into judgment. Facts are often complex, and they present themselves over a period of time rather than all at once. When we decide too quickly, the facts do not line up in the proper order with the correct priority to guide us. I have learned the hard way to force myself, in times of important decision-making, to take "time out" for a day or a month, depending on the situation so God might arrange the facts in an orderly fashion in my heart and mind. When I don't, I often end up kicking myself over misconceptions. When we react too quickly, we let the facts bring us to the wrong conclusions.

We were headed home from Sanubi with three Nigerian student pastors in the backseat, catching a lift back to the pastor's school after another Sunday service in the small Nigerian church where we worshipped each week. It was hot and dusty day in the dry season. Almost too late I caught myself passing a traveler on the roadside. He was moving slowly, legs curled up in paralysis beneath him, a wooden block in each hand, pushing down on the blocks and swinging his torso forward and landing on his buttocks, from where he could again plant the wooden blocks in front of him to swing forward down the dusty road. I was 50 yards beyond him when I stopped and decided to help. Backing up, I got out of the car, as an example to the Nigerian student pastors. Walking over the man who traveled with such fortitude down a road too hot for many to even stroll, I spoke to him about Jesus and gave him the money in my pocket to help him with his needs. Then we drove off, satisfied we had done God's work.

Later that afternoon, God hit me with one of those wooden blocks in the lame man's hands. I had seen the poverty, the brokenness and the difficulty of traveling on one's arms under an extremely hot Nigerian midday sun. I had gathered well all the facts, but I had missed the point. Given the facts as they were, this man's greatest need was not some Nigerian money. *He needed a ride.* In the urgency of the moment, rushing to get myself out of the Nigerian sun, I missed God's best plan altogether. I saw all the facts I needed to make a wise decision, but I did not take the time to order them. Had I taken the time to reflect properly on the information at hand, I would have seen the situation through God's eyes and responded with God's best decision for the moment. Whenever possible, once the facts are gathered, a forced "time out" before making a decision allows time for God the order those facts into His best plan. This is not always possible, but it is often more possible than our emotions would have us think.

Another important factor with time is the pressure caused by the lack of it. Sometimes we are able to make methodical decisions, plotting out all the pros and cons on the notes pages of our smartphones. At other times the decision is urgent, like Todd Beamer's decision on United Flight 93. How do we think of all the right questions and weigh them appropriately when the decision has to be made quickly?

An ophthalmologist friend of mine in another state got up one day to discover his office had somehow double booked him in every slot. He loves the Lord and loves his patients, so he felt the immense pressure of completing the day without making people angry and with his Christian witness intact. He knew it was impossible. It nearly was. Most of us have seen days like that where everything is a rush; there is little time for chitchat or even kindness; our heads are swelling with the pressure. We look back on those days and feel guilty about our attitudes and our ineffective witness for Christ. And so it was with my friend, until the last patient of the day. Hours behind, he saw her with frustration, knowing he had tried before to witness to her for Christ during her illness and she had never been receptive. Unlike many of his impatient patients that day, she greeted him with a smile. "I am so grateful for what you have done for me," she started. "I was going blind and now I can see. And, what's more, I've been thinking about God's place in my life. I did not believe, but now I do."

What a way to end an impossible, time-pressured day. My friend's comment after describing the day was, "No matter how fast you have to go, God can keep up."

And so it is with our time-pressured decisions, "No matter how quickly life forces us to make them, if we are walking in God's will, God can keep up."

Certainly, we should take the time we need to order all the facts when possible, but when not, "God's got this." Move forward with your best guess and trust the Lord whose plan you are completing.

The Fact of Commitment

Many years ago, Becky and I were friends with a much younger Christian couple who were members in our church. We were drawn into their life conversation when the husband was planning to desert his family to follow God's will into ministry— admiral dedication, but he was disconnected from his present commitments. He was so focused on his concept of God's call that he lost the awareness of his responsibility to care for his wife and children. His marriage eventually fell apart when he would not accept his responsibilities for those who depended on him.

All of us carry responsibilities to which we have committed. God uses those commitments to help guide us in our future decisions. We certainly should not feel that all commitments are life long, or that they all have been made with wisdom. There are certainly times we will need to draw away from commitments we made in the past. But if God calls us to do so, He is asking us to do it with honor. Sometimes this means a year's delay in moving down a path God wishes us to follow. Sometimes this involves cost, like losing a year's lease on an apartment, when God says, "Go now." Sometimes it requires letting go of the plan you thought God had made clear to you, realizing other commitments to be the real signpost from God. Commitments may often be anchors to keep us in the garden where God wants us to be planted, when otherwise our impatience or frustration would have us look for a way out of God's best plan. Like any other areas of our lives when we are trying to make a decision, commitments are not the final answer, but they should be respected as we seek to show the world what a Christian looks like.

The God Factor

A word of caution is necessary—God is a fact. We must be careful not to place the other facts we gather as the most important consideration in our decision-making. We are Christians. We know that we do not know all God has in store for us. We do not understand the world as He does, regardless of the extent of our knowledge. Oswald Chambers was wise in his approach to the mathematics of decision-making, "When you reckon things up, bring God in as the greatest factor in your calculations."

We must always leave room for God's knowledge and plans that are far greater and more important than our own. Besides, God's plan may well contradict the path our facts would lead us down.

Young Oswald Chambers loved the Lord, but he also loved the fine arts. He was blessed with wonderful skills and a passion for the field of art. So, based on these facts, he made the decision to enroll in the School of Arts in Edinburgh, Scotland. After initial great success, door after door closed on his future in the art world. Gradually, God began to impress on him the idea of becoming a minister. This did not fit the facts of his life or the passions of his heart. "He didn't see how it was possible. It would mean a complete turnaround from the call he had so confidently followed a year earlier. It would mean abandoning his art studies and leaving the university. Most of all, it would mean exchanging a life-work uniquely suited to his interests and gifts for something to which he had never aspired." (Oswald Chambers: Abandoned to God)

Oswald Chambers had been following God's direction the best he knew how, based on the facts of his skills and passions, for the goal of honoring his Lord. And God told him, "All of these rational concerns are legitimate, but I overrule them. I want you to become a pastor, teach in a Bible college, die of typhoid fever in the deserts of Egypt and have your wife collect your writings to become the greatest devotional book of the 20th century."

Facts are vital, but God often works through revelation that defies our reason. We should always gather the facts, but then we should lay them at the foot of the cross and ask, "This makes sense to me, Lord; does it make sense to you?"

Next Steps

List the facts surrounding your present decision.

Now place the facts in favor of each direction under the column of that direction your decision might take you.

Direction 1   Direction 2   Direction 3

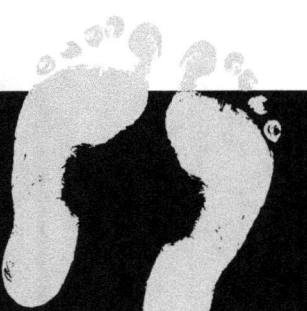

Dear God,
Let me look at these facts with good reasoning. Help me to use them as you will, with your will the most important factor not listed.
Amen

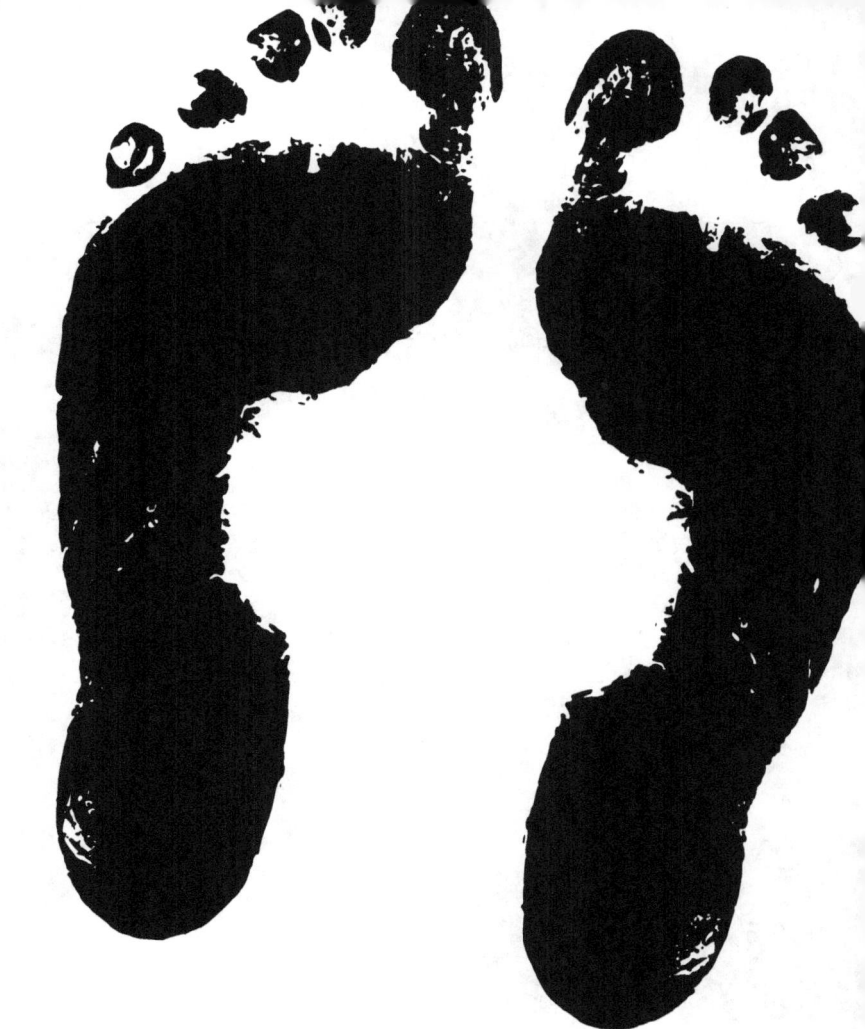

Step Four
Follow His Word

> "Your word is a lamp to my feet
> and a light for my path."
>
> —Psalm 119:105
>
> ---
>
> "Take your Bible and take your newspaper and read both. But interpret newspapers from your Bible."
>
> —Karl Barth

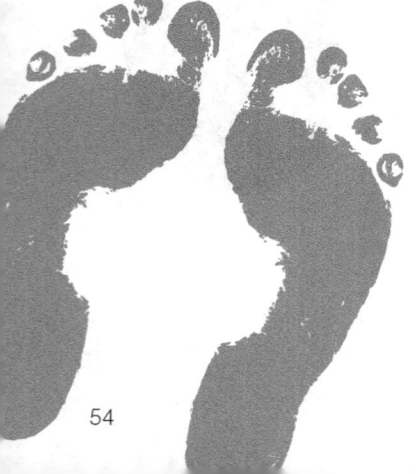

Step Four
Follow His Word

Some folks find ingenious ways to use the Bible, God's Word. Such was the case in Eku, Nigeria. Each morning I made my way to the clinic where patients would line up with their index card medical records. I would pass the large, open air room where, prior to being seen by a physician, the patients sat or stood to hear the message of Christ from our hospital chaplain, Reverend Ujaw. One morning he described the Bible as it had been used in his local village. In his village church, there sat two large Bibles that were never read. But they were useful. Whenever a villager came to know Christ as his Savior, the new Christian would place the Bible on top of his/her head and walk with it to the location of their local juju. They would then take the Bible, blow over the top of it into their juju and then burn the local god.

Though I don't know the depth of meaning of this ritual for these Nigerian Christians, I certainly can imagine the power of God's Word to overcome the idols in our lives. Perhaps we could learn from these villagers.

Most of us use God's Word in other ways to help us in our walk with Christ. How does the Bible really guide us in relationship, acquisition and directional decision-making? So often the specifics of our decisions are not clearly spelled out in Bible pronouncements; and yet, God intends for us to seek Him in His Word. As David said, "Your word is a lamp to my feet and a light for my path" (Psalm 119:105).

God's Word to Choose Targets
We have already mentioned an invaluable method by which the Bible can guide our decision-making: in order for us to choose

wisely our directions in life, we must set our eyes on the optimal targets for our lives. Nowhere else are those targets more clarified than in God's Scripture.

Many years ago, as I was seeking the purpose and direction of my life, a young physician in a busy practice, I attended an evening seminar taught my Mrs. Oral Lee Love. She was a tremendous Bible scholar and was teaching from Dietrich Bonhoeffer's *The Cost of Discipleship*. She reached the story in Matthew 19:16-22 of a rich young man who came to Jesus seeking to gain eternal life. Bonhoeffer's words surrounding that story branded my heart: "When Jesus calls a man, he bids him come and die." Those words, drawn from those verses, drove me to the mission field. And after the mission field became the target of my life, those words drove me to making my life about God's mission rather than mine. Though I have frequently failed and veered from that target, my vision of that target, straight from God's Word, has corrected my course and redefined my decisions throughout my life.

God's Word provides God's best target for our decision-making. For example:

- Target marriage: "Husbands, love your wives, just as Christ loved the church and gave himself up for her" (Ephesians 5:25).

- Target work: "Whatever you do, work at it with all your heart, as working for the Lord, not for men" (Colossians 3:23).

- Target money: "Give to the one who asks you, and do not turn away from the one who wants to borrow from you" (Matthew 5:42).

Target after target is drawn for us as we study God's Word. Shooting for those targets makes many of our decisions along the way crystal clear. Perhaps it is time for many of us to list the short-term and long-term goals of our lives and then place beside them the Scripture to compare them to God's best plan for those targets.

God's Word to Draw Boundaries

God's Word guides us by setting up targets. God's Word also guides our decisions by providing boundaries along our path. As Christians, we are not bound by any law, but the Bible provides clear boundaries within which we should travel.

God provides these boundaries from the depths of His love for us. As Jesus said, "...I have come that they may have life, and have it to the full" (John 10:10). That full life lays within the boundaries God has outlined in His Word. Stepping outside of them may provide transient excitement and pleasure, or even a relief from suffering, but that transient benefit subtracts far more that it adds to the abundant life God planned.

For example, many marriages go through tough times due to the extreme pressures life may bring. Within such times of difficulty, a wife or husband might find sympathetic arms of comfort from a neighbor or co-worker that might lead to intimacy. At the time, within the given circumstance, such intimacy may seem right and justified. But God's Word provides a boundary that protects that marriage from destruction: "You shall not commit adultery" (Exodus 20:14). If such a boundary is honored, the abundant life God plans to bring to that marriage will have a chance to blossom. A decision that might otherwise be difficult to rationalize becomes straightforward based on the boundary laid out in God's Word.

The same goes for countless decisions:

- Should we lie in order to gain a needed promotion at work? (Proverbs 19:22)
- Should we hate someone because they have injured us? (Matthew 5:44)
- Should we keep buying houses larger than we need? (Luke 12:16-21)

These may be extremely difficult decisions in the heat of the moment, but God draws boundaries for us in His Word that allow us to travel down paths toward an abundant life, far more fulfilling than if we walked in the fields outside of His boundaries.

Besides allowing a more abundant life, the boundaries of God's Word also provide us with a more purposeful life. God would have us walk down certain roads, not only that we might receive the maximum blessings in this life, but also that we might best accomplish His purpose as we travel. If I keep building and buying houses greater than I need, the expense of buying and upkeep keep me from serving God with my time and money. If I become angry and shout at someone who has injured me, I lose my right to bear witness for Christ to him. If I lie to my chief of staff in order to gain a promotion, my colleagues see my faith as hypocritical and unworthy to consider.

God's Word with God's boundaries guide us in our decisions so that we might experience both a more abundant life and a more fruitful life.

God's Word for Character

How do we know what kind of men and women God would have us be? God's Word provides the examples we should follow. Most of our decisions grow from who we are in character as much as they do from that which makes best sense in our minds. Character is taught best as example rather than as guidelines to follow. We can acquire such character examples in our daily lives by great men and women we know. We can even read great books and find models to follow. But nowhere can we find greater examples of men and women we should emulate than in the Bible.

- When I read of David and Goliath, I want to be brave (1 Samuel 17).

- When I read the story of David sparing Saul's life near the Crags of the Wild Goats, I want to honor God more than I want to win in this world (1 Samuel 24).

- When I read of David and Jonathan, I want to know loyalty and brotherhood (1 Samuel 20).

- When I read of Job, I learn how to trust as I suffer (Job 42:1-6).

- When I read of Isaiah, I come to grips with my sin in face of our mighty God (Isaiah 6:1-5).

- When I read of Hosea, I want to forgive and accept the forgiveness of God (Hosea 3:1).

- When I read of Peter with Cornelius, I want to accept all men and women as worthy to be loved (Acts 10).

- When I read of the weeping woman, pouring out her expensive perfume to anoint Jesus, I want to give my best to Him (Mark 14:3-9).

- When I read of Paul's ordeals, I want to persevere (2 Corinthians 11:23-27).

- And on and on...

Most of the decisions in my life come from who I am, and much of who I am has been molded by the men and women in God's Word. Character is critical in Christian decision-making, and character is caught as we immerse ourselves in the stories of God's faithful in the Bible.

Unfortunately, for many of us, the great examples we read about in the Bible are stimulating but not transforming. We admire our greatest example, Jesus, for His great character, but go through our lives with little emulation. As Frederick Chan put it:

"You passionately love Jesus, but you don't really want to be like Him. You admire His humility, but you don't want to be THAT humble. You think it's beautiful that He washed the feet of the disciples, but that's not exactly the direction your life is headed. You're thankful He was spit upon and abused, but you would never let that happen to you. You praise Him for loving you enough to suffer during His whole time on earth, but you're

going to do everything within your power to make sure you enjoy your time down here. In short: You think He is a great Savior, but not a great role model."

We might believe that the person we need to become is impossible for us to accomplish, and we are correct. But God does the impossible as He lives His Spirit out through our lives. As we read God's Word, we should seek to become the character we see, rather than becoming an admiring observer. We should then trust in His power, coupled with our determination, to get us there.

God's Word as Presence

For one year I had been struggling with the decision whether to leave my private practice of internal medicine and serve God on the mission field. During my college years I remember standing outside with my father, washing the car and telling him, "I will probably marry Becky and serve on the mission field." No direct action plan came from that conversation. Years later, in December 1980, my wife and I were supervising a group of singles on a weekend Christian retreat at a local state park. That Saturday night, it was dark and the rain was drizzling while Becky and I were outside under a lean-to for concessions. At that moment God filled me with the complete assurance that He wanted us to serve Him in full-time occupational Christian service. I shared this with Becky and we returned home at the end of the retreat to share it with my parents. We did not know where or how God wished us to serve Him within that calling. We prayed for direction, counseled with pastors, considered seminary with no interest in foreign missions, waited, heard nothing and became frustrated. With lack of direction, I signed a three-year office lease and settled back into practice. Confident of my calling, frustrated that life was not steering me in that direction, I opened my Bible and begged for a word. My finger landed on Habakkuk 2:2-3: "Then the Lord replied: 'Write down the revelation and make it plain on tablets so that a herald may run with it. For the revelation awaits an appointed time; it speaks of the end and will not prove false. Though it linger, wait for it; it will certainly come and will not delay.'"

God was present in those verses at that time and told me, "I have not changed my plan. Be patient."

Soon after I discovered the passage above in Habbakuk, I helped organize a church mission meeting where John and Maggie Tarpley, medical missionaries from Nigeria, placed us on the path that eventually carried us to Eku, Nigeria. God had a purpose in our delay: He needed different people and was changing us as we waited. But He also provided His presence within His Word as He delayed us, enabling us to persevere until the course became clear.

God's Word is not a concrete document from which we must discover our direction by sorting out its ancient words. The writer of Hebrews tells us: "For the word of God is living and active..." (Hebrews 4:12).

This was true for the Word that became flesh (John 1:14), and it is true for His Word in the Scripture. God's Spirit is alive within the Bible as we read it, and we can hear the Spirit's whisper if we are sincerely seeking His will for our lives. This passage in Habakkuk that would have meant nothing to me two years before was the very voice of God spoken into my situation in 1981. My method of opening the Bible and sticking my finger on a passage was childish in its despair; but even so, God wanted to speak to me, and He did as He made those ancient words come to life to lead me on.

God's Word as Signpost

William Borden was born into a wealthy American family and one day would have inherited that wealth, but God called him to a life of mission to the Muslim people of Egypt, where he died at the age of 25 from meningitis. His life prior to that was remarkable for his influence on those around him, especially on his colleagues as a student at Yale. His biographer tells the story of William reading God's Word and understanding it as a directional signpost during his college training. After reading the Scripture one morning, he was struck by the verse in

*Matthew 10:32: "Whoever acknowledges me before men, I will also acknowledge him before my father in heaven." Borden felt compelled by this verse to bring an un-churched friend to Bible study. He visited the friend's room, wanting to say something but failed to find the words. The Bible study that evening was centered on Philippians 1:6, "Being confident of this, that he who began a good work in you will carry it on to completion until the day of Christ Jesus." After the study William stood up in the meeting and confessed how he had failed in not witnessing to his friend. He then took courage and again visited his young colleague who was convicted by Borden's invitation to begin to explore the Bible. (*Borden of Yale *by Mrs. Howard Taylor)*

God had sent His Scripture as a signpost toward God's plan to bring his friend to Christ; when he failed, God sent another Scripture to encourage a second try.

God's Word is living and directional. When we continue to abide in His Word, God will post signs to lead us into His right direction, signs that may well be never posted if we fail to read the Scripture.

Jim Elliot was a young man totally committed to the Lord and His direction. He knew God was calling him to His service but spent years searching for the meaning of that call. In July 1950, he was approached by Dave Cooper to join him and a man named Tidmarsh in their work with an unreached people of Ecuador, the Auca Indians. He struggled with the decision, wanting confirmation for the Lord. His diary entry from July 14 describes how God confirmed Cooper's suggestion: "I asked for some word from God ten days ago which would encourage me in going to Ecuador. It came this morning in an unexpected place. I was casually reading in Exodus 23 when verses 20 and 21 came out vividly. 'Behold, I send an angel before thee, to keep thee by the way, and to bring thee into the place that I have prepared. Take heed before him....' Coming as it did (plainly out of context) with such preceding feelings and such simple believing for some promise, I take this as leading from

God that I should write Tidmarsh telling him that I should come to Ecuador in the will of God." Jim followed that leading and served for three years seeking to reach and witness to this very suspicious indigenous population that remained hidden in the depths of the Ecuador forest and had never heard of Jesus. On January 6, 1956, five men made their first contact with the Auca. Two days later, Jim and the other four missionaries were speared to death on a little sand spit on the Curaray River. Their martyrdom launched a ministry that brought countless Aucas to Christ.

Jim Elliot fulfilled God's great plan for redemption of the Auca because he recognized the signpost in God's Word, spoken in the language of his heart.

God is clearly present and alive within His Scriptures. Therefore, as we seek to make important decisions in our lives, we should bury ourselves in His Word on a daily basis and listen to what He has to say.

Next Steps

List all the Scriptures you know that may influence the way you make this decision, whether they be character issues or the clear speaking of God from His Word. Continue to build this list as you move forward in decision-making.

_____
_____
_____
_____
_____
_____
_____
_____
_____
_____

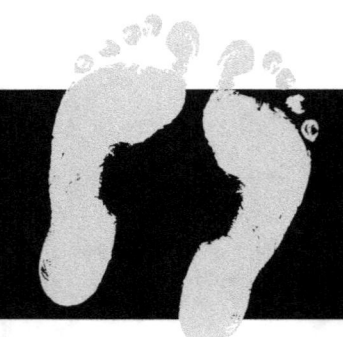

Dear Father,
Please give me a word from your Holy Word. I commit to reading your Word daily until this decision is complete.
Amen

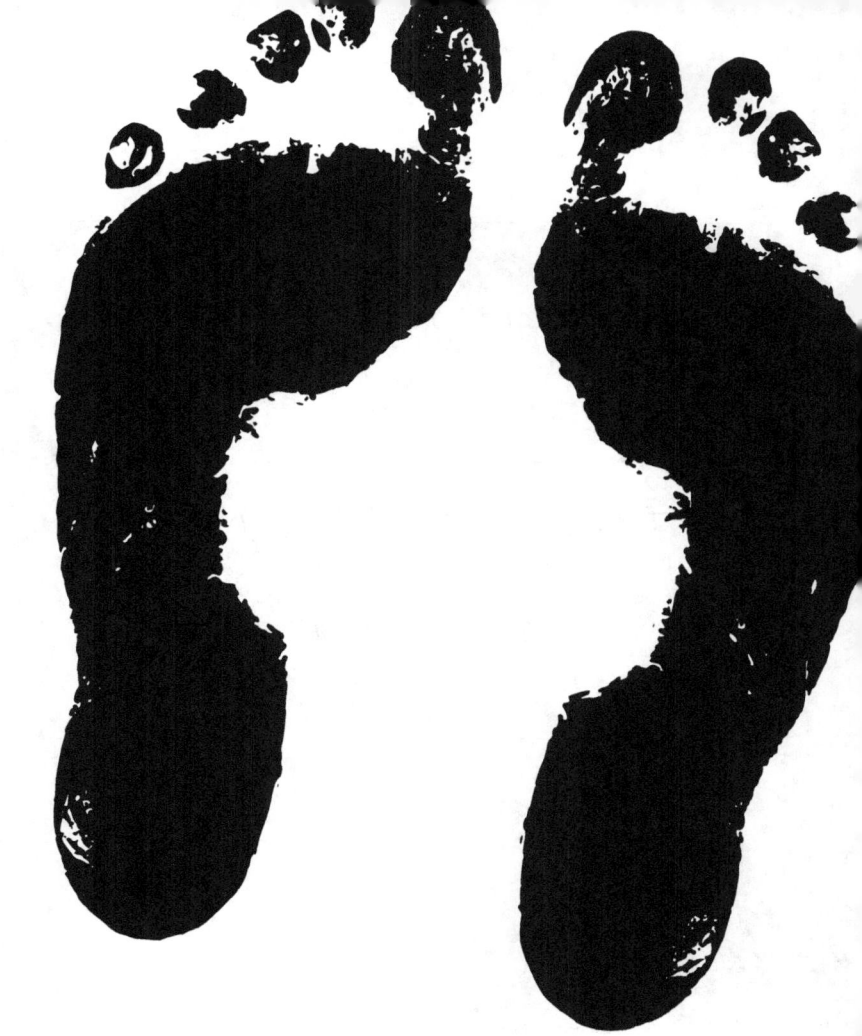

Step Five
Seek Wise Counsel

> "Whatever you have learned or received or heard from me, or seen in me—put it into practice."
>
> —Philippians 4:9a

> "The ideal condition would be, I admit, that men should be right by instinct; but since we are all likely to go astray, the reasonable thing is to learn from those who can teach."
>
> —Sophocles

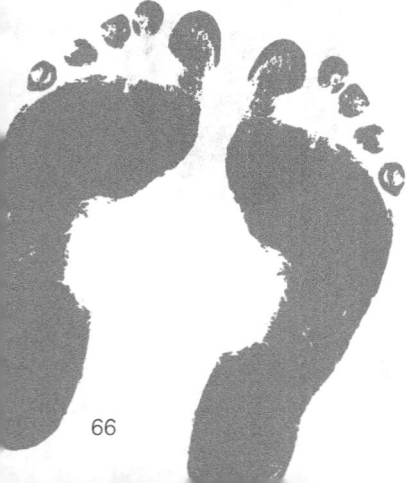

Step Five
Seek Wise Counsel

It was to be the most important decision we would ever make for my grandchildren, and I was only 31 years old.

Becky and I were headed for the mission field, stars in my eyes and a bit of concern in hers. Accepted by the International Mission Board, we were preparing for a life in Nigeria, giving our all for Jesus Christ.

Just prior to leaving for the required seminary training, my wife also developed stars in her eyes as we discovered she was pregnant with our second child. We were ready to move to Seminary Village housing in Louisville, Kentucky and settle in among the future missionaries and pastors of America. And then it all fell apart.

Becky became violently ill with hyperemesis gravidarum, severe morning sickness. She had been fairly sick with our first daughter, but this was much worse in intensity. We had rented our house out and moved in to live with my parents just prior to our departure for Kentucky. I continued my work in the practice of internal medicine. Becky could keep nothing down. Her weakness steadily increased with a total inability to eat in spite of the shots I would give her at home each morning and evening, shots that allowed her to see animals on the walls that no one else could appreciate. She became so debilitated that I eventually had to carry her to the bathroom when she needed to go. Multiple short admissions to the hospital provided only transient relief. Each day I would rush through my work as quickly as possible and sit with her in our small back bedroom, with old television shows playing in black and white, brushing her hair for moments of comfort.

The day came where I began to think I might lose her. The psychiatrist who had failed in his hypnotherapy advised us to abort our baby. Becky was in the hospital making sure it was not a molar pregnancy; the ultrasound demonstrated a beating heart that remains burned into her memory; and the obstetrician agreed to move ahead with the abortion.

We were broken in both emotion and will. We had prayed for healing, as many others had, but healing had not come. We strongly opposed abortion, knowing such action would destroy a child whom God had created with purpose and love. We knew this would end our mission call and might scar us for life, but we were defeated and agreed to the procedure.

The night before the procedure, Becky and I were alone in the hospital room when my father knocked softly and came into the room. His face wore a look of great pain mixed with great love. I don't remember all he said, but I do remember this: "You know I love you, and I know you may never feel the same about me again after this, but I've got to tell you: what you are doing is wrong. You are killing a child."

He left the room. Becky and I fell into each other's arms and sobbed. When our crying ceased, we vowed to keep our child whatever came.

Seven months later, Catherine was born. Two days later Becky and I won the doubles tennis tournament at missionary orientation. Catherine now lives within a mile of us and her four children visit almost every day.

No matter how deep our devotion or how strong our desire to do God's will, we should always make the important decisions in our lives after wise counsel. The key is the word "wise."

Some counsel is wise; some is not.

When Job was suffering intensely, his friends who understood the world surrounded him and advised him as they thought best, but their counsel was far from God's will.

King Saul sought counsel from the witches of Ensor.

Ahab sought counsel from hundreds of prophets of Baal.

David was counseled by Jonathan.

Paul was counseled by Barnabus.

Mary was counseled by Elizabeth.

Some counsel is wise; other is not.

Intelligence and knowledge and even motivation do not guarantee wise counsel. My wife's doctors possessed all of these. "The fear of the Lord is the beginning of wisdom; all who follow his precepts have good understanding..." (Psalm 111:10).

Intelligence, knowledge and motivation are certainly important in advising us toward right decisions, but if they come without an acknowledgment that God is Creator and King, they are less likely to point us toward where we need to be. (Of course, it is also true that folks who know God but are missing intelligence, knowledge and proper motivation will not likely point us where we need to be.) Finding someone with all four is our best chance of finding wise counsel.

We can find such counsel by intently seeking it.

Long after our mission life, when I had been in private practice for a number of years, when our last child was graduating from high school, God began to speak to us about leaving my practice of oncology and moving into occupational Christian ministry. I had a deep hunger in my heart to move in that direction, but I also had some significant questions that needed to be answered. So, I went to my pastor:

- "I'm doing a lot of good where I am, caring for the suffering here. Is it right to leave them behind?"
- "I make a lot of money doing what I do and much of it is

used for God's glory. If I leave my job here, will I lose the ability to serve God in that way?"

- "I have an adventuresome and romantic nature. What if this desire is just that in me, rather than the Lord calling?"

His answers to my questions were wise, and I trusted that he understood my heart. We then spent three great years with student ministry for Christian Medical & Dental Associations. Clearly God's will, clarified with wise counsel.

Wise counsel can be found in other ways. Gatherings of small groups in prayer and Bible study may be the most effective way men and women gain wisdom for decisions in life's daily furnace. Ken Jones, whom I mentioned earlier in this work, shared with me such a small group decision.

This was a group of doctors in Northern California who gathered semi regularly for prayer. While they were praying, word came to them of a child who had been found at the bottom of a swimming pool. She was unconscious in the hospital and not expected to live. Together they made a decision they had never made before. They put down their Bibles and went as a group to the hospital where together they placed their hands on that precious child and prayed for her. The girl was healed. And with that experience, the doctors were changed. Word soon got out that doctors in their community were praying with patients—and the community was changed.

That's the kind of decision I would like to make in my life, but I would rarely do so on my own. Many of us who are not connected to such small groups need to consider finding such support, so God can counsel us with numerous voices.

We can also develop individual relationships that provide ongoing counsel for important decisions in our lives. More and more Christians are finding such relationships through Christian life coaches who help us ask the right questions in order to find the right path. Others establish true mentoring relationships where the mentor not only counsels but also establishes accountability. Both approaches are God-honoring ways to make decisions in all areas of our lives.

Sometimes counsel is caught rather than taught. We don't always have to be spoon-fed wisdom as we are making decisions in life; we can often catch it from observing the actions of those around us.

A bright young female resident shadowed me in clinic today because she was planning to apply for our fellowship program. After we saw a couple of patients, I asked her, "What makes you interested in oncology?" I assumed she would speak of some great healing experience of a family member, as many do who apply for our program. She surprised me with her answer, "My first year as a resident, I was on call when a man who was dying from cancer came into the emergency room. Eric, one of your fellows, came to the ER and took care of him. He sat with the man and talked to him. He couldn't do anything to save him, but for two hours he stayed there, and comforted him, and answered his questions. And then the man died. As I watched Eric's compassion and the peace it brought to that patient's last hours, I wanted to be an oncologist."

This young woman's decision was "caught" from watching, rather than "taught" by listing pros and cons. So many of the major decisions in my life have been influenced in major ways by watching the great men and women I have walked beside. I became a doctor, not only because I loved the science, but because my dad used to take me with him on hospital rounds and drop me off at the nursing station as he visited his patients. I watched his joy at work and wanted that.

I caught God's call as a missionary because I spent time with Dr. John Tarpley and saw the dedication, energy and sacrifice that seemed to flow naturally from his love for Christ. I wanted to live a life like that.

My heart for the downtrodden comes from watching my mother

treat all those she knew with love and without judgment, refusing to hold their choices against them.

I am honest because I have watched those who give back when they are overpaid.

I persevere because of patients who have held their heads up and carried on.

I will probably sit longer at the next bedside of a dying patient because of Eric's example. Watching for wisdom builds a foundation upon which we can layer our rationale thoughts for effective decision-making. Who are you watching?

We can read wisdom, just as we can see it. We reach our highest potential as followers of Christ when we soak ourselves in the stories of Mother Teresa, Eric Liddell, William Wilberforce and Dietrich Bonhoeffer—just as we do when we purposely seek to spend time with those who have handed the direction of their lives to Christ. What are you reading?

Our character grows in the direction of those we spend our time observing. Our decisions then grow out of our character.

And it cuts both ways. Whose character is growing better because they spend their time observing us? Who will make the right decisions in their lives because they watched us make ours?

Next Steps

List three people who love the Lord and might give you good wisdom for your present decisions.

1. _____
2. _____
3. _____

List one great person whose biography you will commit to reading.

1. _____

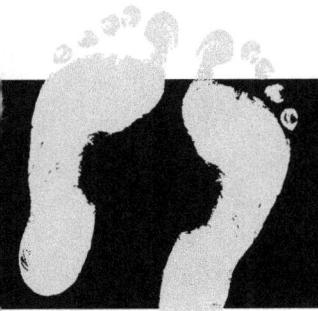

Dear Lord,
I commit to meeting with these three people for wisdom. Please fill them with your Spirit.
Amen

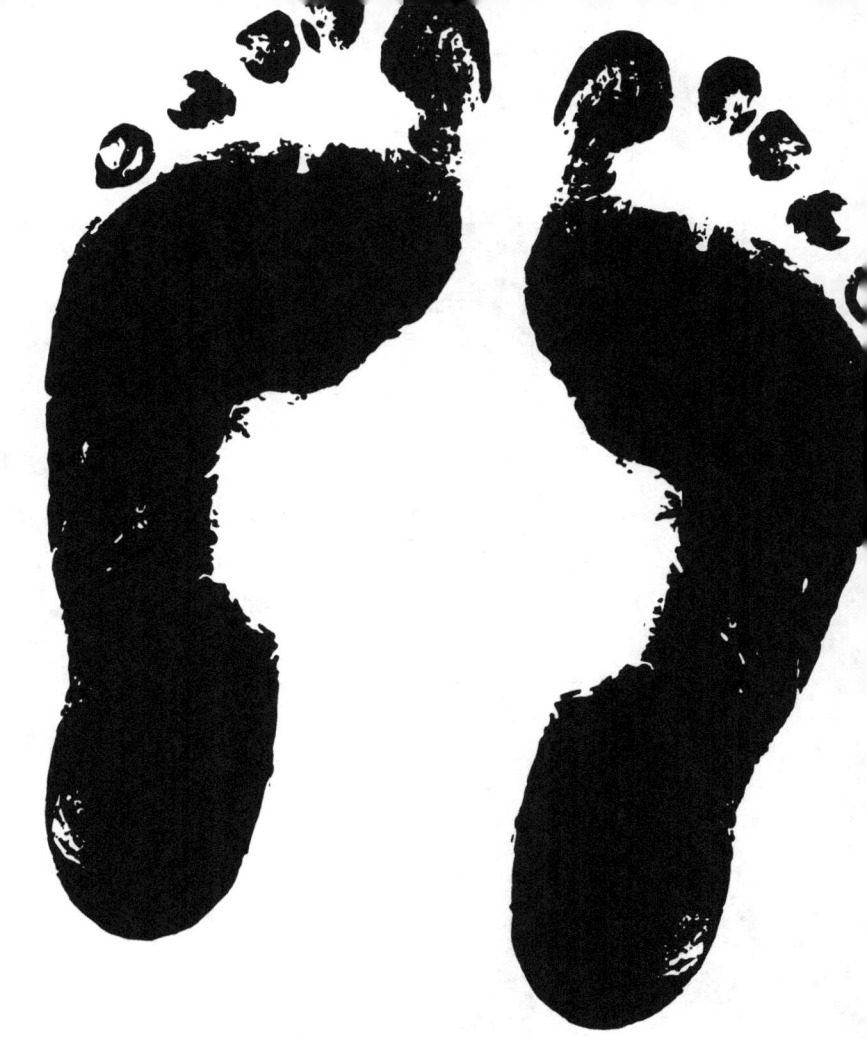

Step Six
Respect Your Passions

> *"Delight yourself in the Lord and he will give you the desires of your heart."*
>
> —Psalm 37:4
>
> ---
>
> *"The future belongs to those who believe in the beauty of their dreams."*
>
> —Eleanor Roosevelt

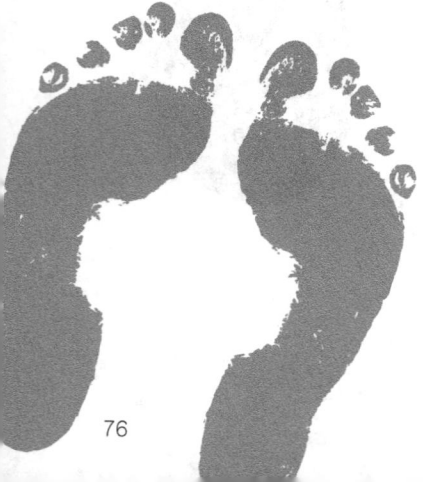

Step Six
Respect Your Passions

Sometimes I wonder why God built me the way I am.

I know He's the one who fashioned my design: "For you created my inmost being; you knit me together in my mother's womb. I praise you because I am fearfully and wonderfully made" (Psalm 139:13-14a).

I know He made me with a purpose in mind: "For we are God's workmanship, created in Christ Jesus to do good works, which God prepared in advance for us to do" (Ephesians 2:10).

Some things about me I wish were different, but mostly because I've got my plans in mind, not His. I have the body God gave me, with all of its warts, with all of its amazing design. I have the family I was born into, the culture and country He placed me within, the mind, the emotional framework. Much of this was God-designed for the work He prepared for me to do in this world for Him.

I also have the passions He built within me for His purpose. I certainly have the passions I myself created from within my sinful desires, passions of pride and greed, etc., but woven within my fabric of being are the passions God gave me to do His will. So, when I make important decisions in my life, I should respect those God-given passions in my decision-making.

Eric Liddell was a great man of God who served his Lord and died as a missionary for Christ in China during World War II within a Japanese internment camp. Most of us know him best for his commitment to the Sabbath portrayed in the beautiful movie Chariots of Fire. *In addition to his devotion to our God, Eric was a great runner. They called him The Flying Scotsman. The movie described his selection by Great Britain to run in the Olympics in Germany in 1924. He was selected to run the 100-meter race, which was his best chance of winning the gold medal. But before he left for Germany, he discovered that the qualifying race was to be run on a Sunday. Eric was committed to keeping the Sabbath as a day of rest, and that precluded him from running in an Olympic qualifying round on that day. All the pressure of the British Empire was placed across his shoulders, but he did not give in. Instead, he sacrificed his best chance of a medal and was forced to compete in a race he had not planned to run. He won gold in the 400-meter race—and God demonstrated his approval by that victory.*

One beautiful scene in Chariots of Fire *points to an important principle in our own decision-making. In this scene, Eric Liddell is having a private conversation with his sister who is begging him to give up the running that she feels is superficial compared to his plans to join her in China as a missionary. Eric replies to her entreaty, "God made me for China and one day I will be there, but God also made me fast, and when I run, I feel God's pleasure."*

With this understanding, Eric made a decision that ultimately broadcasted his faithfulness to millions of people through his widely publicized story. God created within Eric Liddell the passion to run, and Liddell respected that passion to the glory of God.

Sometimes those who most love Christ feel that we should sacrifice all we might enjoy in this world so that Christ might be best served. But this is often not the case. Sacrifice is essential to completing God's task for which we have been each created; but, when we give our all to Jesus, He hands much of it back to us for *His use through us* in the world. Often, the things that make our heart most joyful are the things He hands back to us with an annotation: "This is no longer yours; take it and use it for me." Pursuing the passions that give us such pleasure in life may well be the direction through which He guides us in many of our important decisions.

When I was a third year internal medicine resident, I had established a fellowship-training program in cardiology and was headed that direction when I entered a rotation in hematology. And there my life changed. Dr. Luther Burkett was a one-armed hematologist who served as my faculty that month. Bone marrow aspirations are difficult for two people to complete. With his one arm he could not only perform the procedure, but he could also suck the marrow, lay down the needle and smear the specimen perfectly on a slide before it clotted. I am still amazed. Dr. Burkett's love for hematology was contagious. By the end of the month I was hooked. I have not ceased loving the subject in the decades since. I have no doubt that much of God's work through me was planned before I was born and has depended on my love for hematology.

God creates us and forms us after our birth with certain great desires in our hearts that fulfill us personally. I suspect that, most often, God wants us to pursue those passions as part of His plan for our lives. We know we work best when we work on something we love; God knows that as well and plans that for His glory.

Frederick Beuchner wrote, "The place God calls you to is the place where your deep gladness and the world's deep hunger meet."

Of course, this is not always true. Oswald Chambers (whose teaching led to the world's greatest daily devotional, *My Utmost for His Highest*) loved art and wished to spend his life as an artist. Instead, God directed him to become a Bible teacher.

Likewise, Dr. Joshua Bogunjoko, the International Director for SIM (Serving in Mission), warns us, from his own experience, against taking our hearts' desires and placing them in the driver's seat of our lives rather than the passenger seat. When he grew up in rural Nigeria, he wanted to make something of himself for his family. He loved math and felt that God would therefore let him be an engineer. And then God began to make it clear He wished for Joshua to become a doctor. Dr. Bo-

gunjoko said he held an ongoing argument with God, "I hate hospitals. I hate becoming a doctor. You, God, should like for me what I like." Of course, God knew best. Joshua became a missionary doctor for Christ and now loves where God has placed him, with the profession he thought he would hate.

Thus, we can't always depend on our passions to be the chief compass for direction finding. That which fulfills our hearts' desire most may or may not be the signpost for our next decision in life. But these passions must be respected and analyzed with God's guidance.

How do we decide if our passions line up with God's direction?

1. Take them seriously as God given and God desired.
2. Give them back to the Lord as an offering to do as He wishes for His glory.
3. Imagine how the fulfillment of our passions might bring redemption to the world and glory to our Creator.
4. Examine our lives for any sin, including that of pride that might have attached itself to our seeking our passion.
5. Fit these passions within the context of the other twelve steps we have listed in this book, including wise counsel, God's Word, prayer, earthly circumstances, relationships and the other steps we are discussing.

If our passions fit within these guidelines and we move forward toward fulfilling our passion, we then need to continually ask the motive question, "As I do this, is it for self-fulfillment or God's glory?" As we do so, we must understand that choosing God's glory over self-fulfillment is always necessary, but it does not necessarily require throwing away that which brings us our greatest joy. In fact, it is far more likely God will have us turn in the direction of our greatest joys than away from them as we choose to do His will. If God chooses another direction, we can be confident He will replace that which we felt was most important with that which far more fulfills the desires of our hearts.

So, as you make the next big decision in your life, respect your passions, hold them up to God and say, "You made me to love this pursuit in my life. If it is your will, let me continue to pursue it, but I give it up to you; use it as you will. How now do I fit this passion within the decision I am about to make?"

Next Steps

List the things in life that your heart really draws you toward. Examine them with the five guidelines. Erase those that are clearly not in God's will for your life.

_____
_____
_____
_____
_____
_____
_____
_____
_____

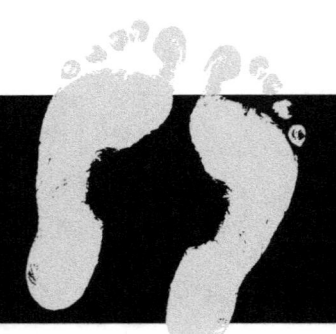

Dear Father,
You have made me this way, with these great desires. I give them to you. Take them and use them or remove them from my life.
Amen

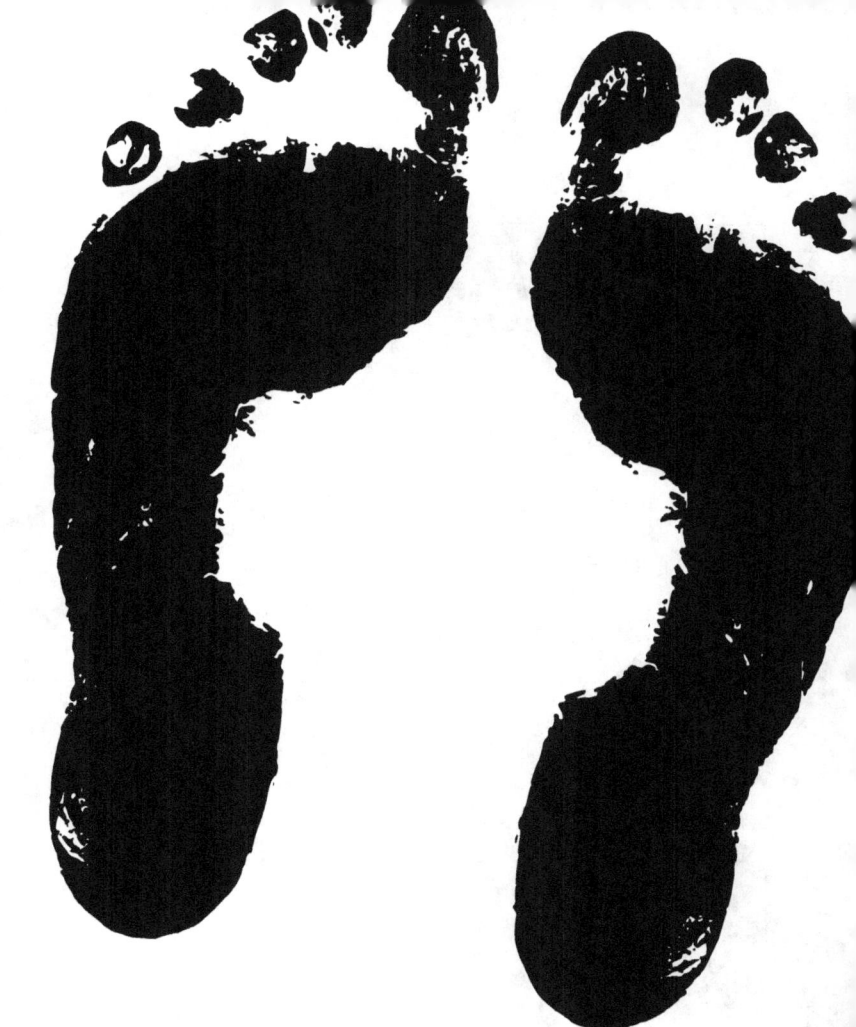

Step Seven
The Centrality of Abiding

> "If you abide in me, and my words abide in you, ask whatever you wish, and it will be done for you."
>
> —John 15:7, ESV

> "God will answer all our questions in one way and one way only, namely by showing us more of his son."
>
> —Watchman Nee, *The Normal Christian Life*

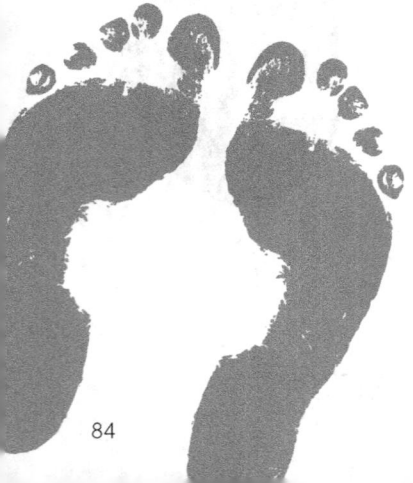

Step Seven
The Centrality of Abiding

I have been blessed twice in my life to hear Joni Eareckson Tada speak at conferences, and once to sit at the banquet table with her. Joni is an amazingly talented woman, deeply committed to Jesus, who was paralyzed from the shoulders down as a teenager. From within her ongoing suffering, she has been able to speak a message of faith, perseverance and surrender to Jesus that comes from the authority of one tested by fire. Because of her physical disability, others who are disabled and need advice often contact Joni. During my first opportunity to learn from her, she told a story of decision-making that has never left me.

A few years ago, Joni shared the story of a young woman with amyotrophic lateral sclerosis whose paralysis was progressing over many months. The paralysis would soon weaken her chest to the point she would no longer be able to breathe on her own. She thus had the decision before her whether to depend on an artificial ventilator for the rest of her life or to let go and die. This young woman was a Christian. Joni visited the woman in her own wheelchair and was overcome with the profound nature of the decision and her inability to help the young woman make such a difficult call with such profound outcomes. Sitting next to this girl, Joni had no answers, and therefore began to softly sing the only direction she could give:

*"I must tell Jesus all of my trials;
I cannot bear these burdens alone.
In my distress He kindly will help me;
He ever loves and cares for His own.
I must tell Jesus! I must tell Jesus!
I cannot bear my burdens alone.
I must tell Jesus! I must tell Jesus!*

Jesus can help me, Jesus alone."
(Elisha Hoffman, 1893)

I do not know the young woman's ultimate decision, but Joni's message was clear: if we are followers of Christ, the only safe place to be with our decisions is right next to Jesus.

Jesus shared this same message with His disciples just before the cross: "I am the vine; you are the branches. If a man remains in me and I in him, he will bear much fruit; apart from me you can do nothing" (John 15:5).

Our Lord was saying that we are to be linked to Him as a branch to a vine, dependent on Him for our strength, nourishment and direction in life. And, ultimately, it's all about fruit. Whether we choose to let Jesus' statement fit into the process of our decision-making depends on whether *fruit* has anything to do with our decisions.

But, you say, "This isn't a religious decision. I need to decide which job to take. I need to know whether to marry this guy. I need to know whether to sell my lake house and give it to the poor. What's fruit got to do with it?"

We need to go back and consider the long-term targets for our lives. At the foundation of every decision should be my desired outcome for this life. The central question in every decision I make is whether I choose to accomplish God's purpose for my life. Do I choose to produce the fruit that honors Him, or do I choose to seek first my self-fulfillment? Jesus is telling us, regardless of the immediate decision that needs to be made, we cannot accomplish His purpose for our lives unless we abide with Him. Superficial goals can be accomplished on our own, but God's great redemptive purpose that speaks through all of our decisions requires our abiding in Christ.

Only by abiding do we understand who we are: children of the King, adopted by grace, powerless to make life eternally worthwhile without Him.

Only by abiding do we understand who He is: Creator and King of the universe with the heart of Jesus—a heart of love with no sacrifice too great to prove it; a heart of power with no mountain too hard to climb; a heart with knowledge unlimited.

When we walk with Jesus, we begin to listen to Him, and we begin to think like Him.

> *Over the last few years, I have had the painful and blessed privilege of watching my son move away from home and make a new life with the wonderful woman he loves. I have seen him drawn more and more to know Christ and be like Him. Two years ago, when he moved to his new home a few hundred miles away, my wife Becky and I helped them move. While we were in their new town near Mobile Bay, we thought what a great idea it would be for him to have a small bay boat, so he and his wife could enjoy the water and the fish that were waiting for his dinner table. After discussions and sincere prayer, we went 50:50 purchasing a small boat. He has loved it, fishing in the bay and into the Gulf, spending days in the sun with his wife, taking friends and family into the sun-filled beauty. Three months ago, I received a surprise letter from him. He had sold the boat and was sending me back my part of the money. It was for him a God honoring decision. As he had drawn closer and closer to Jesus, he began to listen to Him, began to think like Him. There was nothing wrong with owning a boat; the boat was a good thing. But time with Jesus had convinced our son he was spending too much time and too much money enjoying his time on the water when Jesus would have him use the same time and money to focus on a better plan.*

My son never asked me about that decision, but I have never doubted its wisdom because I know it was made out of a deep abiding relationship with Christ.

The neat thing about abiding in Christ is that it relieves much of the pressure of decision-making. "What if I get it wrong?" is often in our heads. We seek fervently a clear message from God and find nothing in our heads but common sense.

We come to decision-making points where time has run out, and the decision must be made "now," and the answer is still not clear. Where do we go from here?

When we reach the necessary decision time with no clear answer, these words of Oswald Chambers are incredibly freeing: "If we are saved and sanctified, God guides us by our everyday choices... The disciple who abides in Jesus is the will of God, and what appear to be free choices are actually God's foreordained decrees."

Wow.

"The disciple who abides in Jesus *is* the will of God."

If our goal is God's will, we can't get any closer than this. Seek with the best process I can and then take the step that seems most right when the decision must be made. The pressure is off—if I am abiding.

So, how do we do it? How do we abide in Christ in a way that makes our decisions into God's decisions? Most of us know how; we just don't do what we know.

We know to spend time each day with Jesus in prayer. Do we?

We know to seek our Lord in His Scripture each day. Do we?

We know we can find Jesus in worship. Do we?

We know Jesus is present when His followers gather for study and discussion; there we can hear Him in the voices of those who follow Him. Do we gather with other Christians regularly and share the Christ within us? Do we rest in His Holy Spirit?

Rupert's voice was still quite hoarse after completing radiation for a laryngeal cancer 18 months ago. Before his cancer, he had been quite a vocalist, writing and singing Christian music, some of which I enjoyed from CDs he had given me. The struggles he endured had not dampened his musical spirit; he was still writing and singing, now with a unique raspy voice. As we finished his office visit, he told me about a new song he had written and was going to perform in church as a duet with an 8-year-old girl the next Sunday. "It's a beautiful song about the Holy Spirit," he said. His wife chimed in, "My favorite line in the song is 'We can't see the air we breathe, but we know it gives us life.'"

"We can't see the air we breathe, but we know it gives us life."

It gives us life when we abide.

I rarely give God's Spirit enough credit in my life. I certainly acknowledge His power in my prayers and pray for His help in times of trouble...but most of the time I act out my life as if God depended on me, rather than the other way around.

The truth is: there is actually very little that God depends on me to do.

The *plan* for our lives and each of our steps is decided by His Spirit.

The *power* to accomplish anything of value in our lives comes from His Spirit.

The *results* of all our actions for His kingdom are His responsibility.

"We can't see the air we breathe, but we know it gives us life."

What then is left for us? What is our responsibility as we live for His kingdom?

Our task is but to abide, to listen, to obey and to trust.

We must *listen* hard and seek His guidance.

We must *obey* whenever we feel His leading.

We must *trust* Him for direction, power and outcomes.

But it is all His plan, His power and His results.

We access that plan, power and results by abiding in Christ.

"We can't see the air we breathe, but we know it gives us life."

Abiding is vital in our attempt to find God's best direction for important decisions. But what if we don't feel like abiding? What if God is distant right now? What can I do to get back that feeling of His presence? I remember the time He seemed so close I could almost hear Him speak, but not now.

Such is the experience for all Christians at some time in our lives. These times of separation come with over-work and time pressure. They come with a prolonged focus on self-realization through acquiring and doing. One day we wake up and realize our best friend, Jesus, is not around. So we try to shock ourselves back into relationship by reading the right book, showing up for more church, listening to spiritual tapes, volunteering for work at a free clinic...all good, all self-initiated shocks to restart our hearts for God. And yet, nothing we do seems to bring back that feeling of closeness to God.

Then, in the middle of a fast-paced day, an elderly woman speaks a word of grace, or a bumper sticker hits us right between the eyes; and God sweeps into our lives and we are home with Him again. Go figure.

It's all God. We cannot shock ourselves back to Him when we feel we have drifted away. It was He who found us in the first place, and He has not let us go.

So, are our attempts at seeking to renew that relationship simply wasted? I don't think so. I suspect God wants very much for us to seek Him with all the efforts of community, worship and service. And, as we do, He will honor our seeking by erasing the gap we fashioned, allowing us to realize His never-absent presence again.

Prayer

A special word needs to be said about prayer and decision-making. Prayer is vital. But prayer as a business model, prayer as a way to accomplish what we want, is less important than prayer as a way of abiding. Praying hard that God will do what we ask is important (Mark 11:24). But, in decision-making, the most valuable benefit of prayer is the time spent with the One we love, so that our will may become one with His.

Prayer at its best is a way of seeking Christ and abiding with Christ; and, just as we open our hearts and pour out our desires to our best friends, prayer is that opening and pouring out that comes naturally within an intimate relationship. Then, just as we would do our all to answer the heart of the One we most love, so will our God do His all to answer us as we open ourselves to Him. Our prayers toward decision-making are just such endeavors.

This world is extremely hectic, and it is easy to slip away from the awareness of His presence. Very often in the midst of fast-paced living, I pray again my morning prayer:

"Let me rise up and meet You and empty myself for You; fill me, so that the lost may be found in You, the broken made whole in You and that You may be glorified."

And with this prayer, I sense the presence of God in the room and refocus my decisions on His plan rather than my own.

If we are going to get it right with most of our decisions, right in a way that really matters in eternal ways, abiding in Christ must be central.

Again, from Oswald Chambers: "The questions that matter in life are remarkably few and they are all answered by the words, 'Come to Me.'"

Next Steps

Which one practice on this list do I perform least well and commit to improving, so I might more closely abide in Christ?

1. Daily prayer.
2. Daily reading God's Word.
3. Meeting regularly to discuss my faith with other Christians.
4. Meeting regularly to worship.
5. Stopping at least twice in the middle of my day and asking Christ to continue with me.

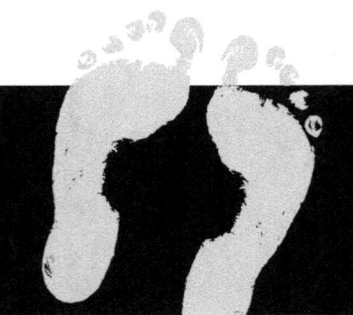

Dear Father,
I commit to time with you every morning and time with you every evening until this decision is made. Help me also to know your presence in the middle of my busy day.
Amen

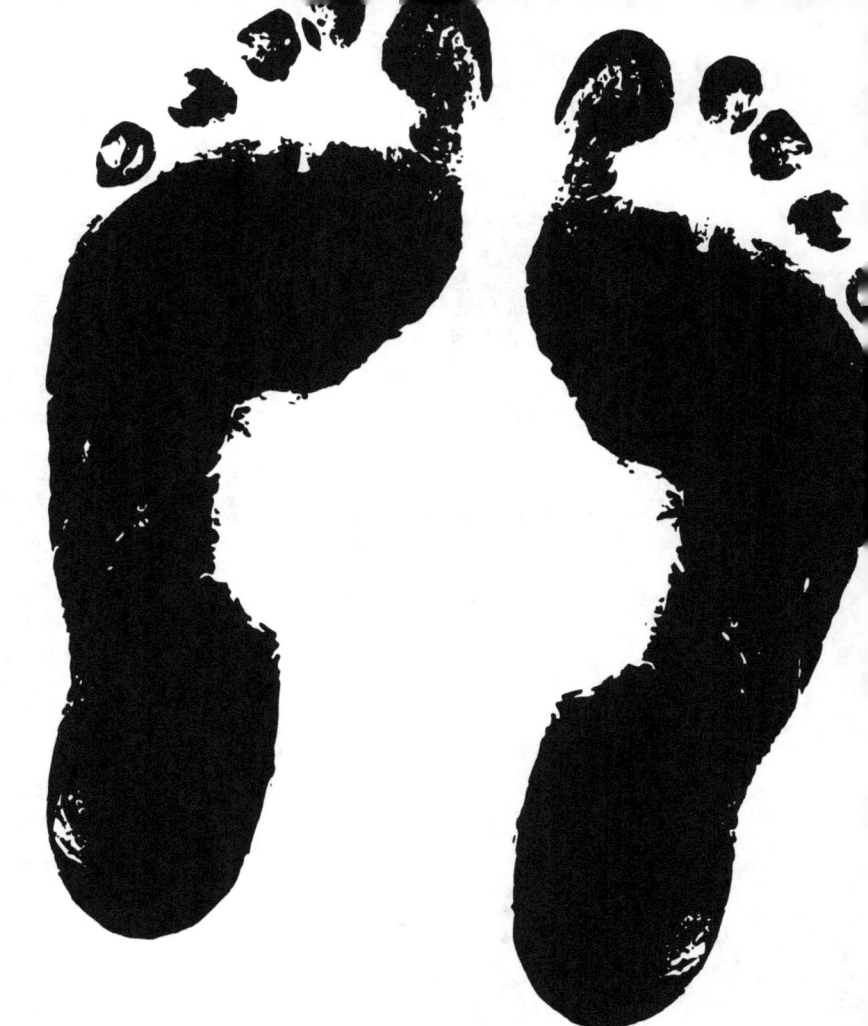

Step Eight
Listen Hard

> "You will seek me and find me when you seek me with all your heart."
>
> —Jeremiah 29:13
>
> ---
>
> "The voice is dangerous for the happy when they have the courage to listen for it."
>
> —Albert Schweitzer

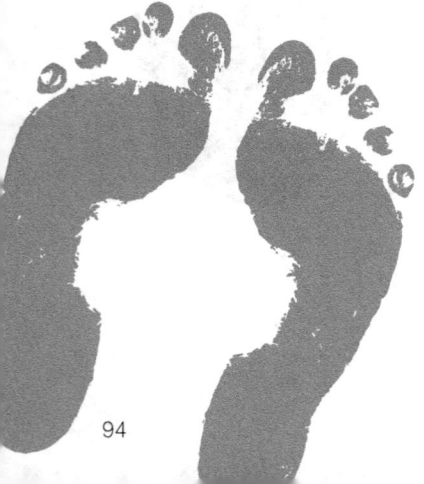

Step Eight
Listen Hard

We had arrived the day before, jet-lagged strangers in a strange land covered with palm trees, mango and heat. As we were putting our house together within the hospital compound, a guest arrived. The king of the nearby town of Abraka had come to greet us and bring my first patient. His wife had been ill for many weeks and no one had been able to determine the cause. I was the new internal medicine specialist from the United States and worth a try.

In my evaluation I discovered a number of facts. She had been suffering from fevers for many weeks and was becoming more and more lethargic. She had no visible active infection but had an enlargement of her lymph nodes, especially behind her ears. The rest of her history and physical examination was normal. I had no idea what was wrong with her. Being the brilliant doctor I was, I took my tropical medicine textbook and flipped through the pictures to look for any similar illnesses. And there it was, a picture of an African woman with sleepy eyes and enlarged lymph nodes behind her ears. Eureka. The king's wife must have trypanosomiasis, African Sleeping Sickness. I discussed this with my colleagues and discovered my diagnosis was impossible since there was no such disease in this part of Nigeria. Nevertheless, it was the only diagnosis I could come up with, so I followed the book to prove it. First step was to stick a needle in a lymph node, squirt the juice on a slide and look for the trypanosomes. I was good with a microscope, but I searched the lymph juice forever and found nothing. So, I doubled down. I asked my surgical colleagues to take out a node. I took that lymph node, cut it in half and then squeezed the juice onto a microscope slide. I must have looked for 10 minutes, straining my eyes in the scope and nothing was visi-

ble. I rested my eyes and then searched again, hoping to see what I had never seen before—and then a lymphocyte moved, and then another, and then I saw the tail wiggling frantically, and then I saw the trypanosomes everywhere.

It took forever to find that first trypanosome, but we did, and the king's wife was cured of her illness. By the time we screened all the people in his town for the disease, we discovered 67 cases of trypanosomiasis in an area where it had never been reported. A fascinating outcome was the skill I developed in seeing the trypanosomes under the microscope. Though the first case took hours to find, by the time we saw the 67th, I could spot trypanosomes immediately when I looked at a slide.

The more we seek, and the harder we seek, the easier it is to find. For some reason, God wants us to seek Him hard, to look hard for Him in the world, to listen hard for His whisper in the world. It has something to do with His wanting our hearts.

"You will seek me and find me when you seek me with all your heart" (Jeremiah 29:13).

"But if from there you seek the Lord your God, you will find him if you look for him with all your heart and with all your soul" (Deuteronomy 4:29).

God is present in our lives, and He is speaking to us in our world. He wants us to find Him, and He wants us to know His will for our lives. But for some reason, and possibly because He wants our hearts to yearn for Him, God often walks in shadows and often speaks in whispers. If we do not intently seek Him, if we do not listen hard, we may not see Him clearly and hear from Him His will for our lives.

Israel's prophet, Elijah, knew the whisper of God. After his great victory over Ahab's prophets, he had run in fear from Jezebel's wrath. When he was hiding in a cave, the Lord came to him: "The Lord said, 'Go out and stand on the mountain in the presence of the Lord, for the Lord is about to pass by. Then a great and powerful wind tore the mountains apart and shattered the rocks before the Lord, but the Lord was not in the wind. After the wind there was an earthquake, but the Lord was not in the earthquake. After the earthquake came a fire, but the Lord was not in the fire. And after the fire came a gentle whisper" (1 Kings 19:11-12).

And that whisper was the voice of God.

So often when we are seeking God's direction for an important decision in our lives, we want badly to feel the earth tremble and the see the sky light up God's message before us. But, for most of our lives, God speaks in whispers and walks in shadows. We must look hard and listen hard with our whole hearts to find His will.

Ultimately, it is a matter of focus. If we are to recognize Jesus in the decision that presently demands our focus, we must learn to find Him first in many other directions. Where do we focus our eyes and ears and minds and hearts to find Jesus?

Our focus on the Lord involves our whole lives and is necessarily multidirectional.

We must focus *on our past*, that we might know to the depths of our being that we are sinners for whom Jesus died and washed us clean.

We must gaze *into our future*, where Jesus is calling, into eternity, into a life of mission, into a decision that needs to be made. We must never forget that any present decision must be consistent with the mission to which God has called us.

I love Albert Schweitzer's description of that call in *Search for the Historical Jesus*: "He comes to us as One unknown, without a name, as of old, by the lake-side, He came to those men who knew Him not. He speaks to us the same word: 'Follow thou me!' and sets us to the tasks that He has to fulfill for our time. He commands. And to those who obey Him, whether they be wise or simple, He will reveal Himself in the toils, the conflicts, the sufferings which they shall pass through in His fellowship, and as an ineffable mystery, they shall learn in their own experience Who He is."

And our focus must not only be on our past and into our future; our focus must be ever *upward*. God is on His throne. He is in charge. Our present decisions are important to our little story in life, and they are also important to His great redemptive story. Any decision we make now must lie within that story God is writing for the history of His creation.

We must focus backward, forward, upward and absolutely *inward*, where Christ is. For only He should be glorified in the decisions we have before us. Only by abiding in Him and listening to Him can we move forward for His glory.

We have work to do. We must train our eyes and ears to be constantly focused backward, forward, upward and inward for His voice and presence. Only then can we can best discern His whisper when we focus *outward* into our world, to the decision we need to make, to the people and actions around us, where God is working, where God is calling, within a noisy, crowded world.

How does that work out? Sometimes it is true that we see the fire or feel the earth quake and know clearly the direction in which God is sending us. I have been there, but most of the time it is not that way in my life. Most of the time, if our hearts are truly seeking Him, we will discover His will as nudges, as unexplained confidence along the pathway we are entering. But it takes a listening ear and intent eye, a genuine desire to follow such road signs.

Jennifer had been my patient for a number of years and was nearly healed from a recent problem. She loves the Lord and knows that I do as well. Before I could ask her about her health one visit, she interjected, "First, I've got to tell you the neatest story. I was taking my sons to Dunkin' Donuts yesterday. When I walked in, I saw a very thin and dirty guy at the door and thought, 'That man looks hungry.' I didn't do anything about it because I was in a hurry—paid for my donuts, got in my car and started to drive off. But God kept nudging me that I should give this man something to eat. I tried to avoid the message, because I was in a hurry, but God kept nudging me. So I switched from 'reverse' to 'drive' and pulled back into a parking space. As I was getting ready to open the door, this waiter knocked on my window with a bag in his hand 'You forgot your sausage and egg biscuit.' I told him I had not ordered a sausage and egg biscuit and he said, 'Well, you might as well take it.' I got the message and told him, 'No, go give it to that man over there.' I simply obeyed God's nudge and God made the sandwich."

Jennifer "got the message" because she is one who listens hard each day of her "normal life." She got the message as nudges from God, as many of us do. The question is whether we are too desensitized by our personal busyness and pressures to feel the nudges of God.

Listening hard applies most directly to our prayer life:

I was praying my usual prayers during my run that morning, going down a list of many I had been holding up to the Lord. When I came to Roland's name, God stopped me. The week before I had sent Roland to a residence hospice for end-of-life care. I had not spoken to the family since. God spoke within my prayers, "You need to get out there and see him." I did that day and was able to spend time with Roland's family on his last day this side of Glory.

Have we practiced the discipline of listening when we pray? At the end of our daily prayers, do we sit still a few moments and let God speak before we rush into our day or slip into our nightly dreams?

Who knows what God might tell us?

It's actually a scary thought to think that God might rearrange our lives should we truly listen to Him. I'm not sure I'm ready for that. I know that, when Jesus spoke, James and John "...left their father Zebedee in the boat with the hired men and followed him" (Mark 1:20); and I know that Levi got up from his tax collector's booth to follow Jesus into a rearranged life (Mark 2), but I'm not sure I'm ready for that. So, I'm not sure I want to stop my day for a few minutes at the conclusion of my usual requests and listen to what God has to say.

Many of God's "nudges" to me have been realized during prayer:

Not so long ago, I made a home visit to a patient I had not seen for a while. It was a spur of the moment decision that came up on a light weekend. I had been praying for him and just felt it was a good day to follow up on my prayers. Today his wife spoke to me and told me how important that visit had been for Jon, "Just before you came, Jon had spoken to me and told me: he said that my daughter and I would be better off without him and his chronic illness. He said we could then get on with our lives without him as a constant burden. He then went into his room for a nap. I prayed, 'If only the doctor would come by,' and you did."

I had no idea Jon was in a crisis moment before I visited him, but I showed up, following a consciousness birthed in prayer.

We so much wish for God to show us signs to lead us in right directions. We want to see and understand and become confident that we are headed in the right direction.

But, the longer I live and seek God's direction for my life, the less I think I need to hear or understand it clearly in order to be right where He wants me.

With years and years of asking God to place me within His will, I have become convinced that my heartfelt desire to be in His will and the straining of my eyes and ears to see and hear Him is often far more necessary than my understanding clearly where to go. If I seek His will with all my heart, listen hard and plan to obey when I am allowed to see it, I am confident He will place me there, sometimes with clarity and other times just blind and trusting.

Nudging and impressing:

Fred came up to me after a Bible study and grabbed me by the sleeve.

"Can I tell you something that happened this week?"

"Sure."

"For the last two weeks, God has really been impressing on me that I should be witnessing for Him more each day. On Thursday, I had finished taking care of one of my elderly patients and was about to leave the room, when I just felt compelled to turn back to him. I asked him, 'Would you mind if I asked you if I could pray with you?' He looked up with me with tears in his eyes, 'No one has ever prayed with me before.' He cried, and I cried and then we prayed. God led me to that man."

God did not speak with thunder or write His message across the wall to encourage Fred to turn back into that room. Fred turned back to share God's love with that elderly man because God had been "impressing" on him. And Fred was listening hard.

If nudging and impressing is not enough, God will use whatever language we need.

Dr. Gene Rudd rarely shares his stories from Rwanda. They are too deep and too dark for most us to comprehend. He was serving in Kigali with Samaritan's Purse to keep a hospital open during the genocide when God threw him into an experience that has become central to my understanding of our place in God's redemptive mission. In the midst of the killing time, Gene was caring for a patient with Shigella pneumonia. Buried beneath 20-hour days of patching up the victims of untold cruelty, Gene had been focused intensely on his work of healing. One day, as he was looking into the eyes of this dying patient, God's Spirit reawakened him to his true purpose within the tragedy. Unable to speak the man's language, and knowing the man and his family understood no English, Gene searched for his interpreter but was unable to track him down. Compelled by God's Spirit, desperate to share words of life with this dying man, Gene sat down with the patient and his family and began to share the gospel in English. When he had completed sharing God's truth from his heart, Gene held hands with the man, his wife and his daughter and prayed a prayer of salvation. One hour later the man died. When Gene located his interpreter, he asked him to go and comfort the woman and explain the message he had tried to convey. The interpreter did so and reported their response back to Gene: "How did the doctor know our language?" They had listened to the words Gene spoke in English and heard God speak to them in their own language. Even more vitally, the wife, the daughter and the patient had each accepted Christ as their Savior as Gene had held their hands and prayed.

If we want His will and listen hard, God will speak as clearly as necessary in the language we need to help us take the next step. One language God loves to use is Scripture.

I was walking briskly onto the hospital grounds in the center of Tirana, with Mount Deiti rising above me on my left. At the entrance to the hospital the beggars lined up. Some were but small children, beautiful and desperate, others were old men, smoking their cigarettes, eyes squinting in blindness. It did not occur to me that I should help these few on my way to the sea of broken bodies waiting inside the hospital—until I passed the last one. Then God spoke. "Give to the one who asks you..." (Matthew 5:42). I was ashamed that my Lord had to remind me about that which I had known for so long. On my way back, headed for my nice hotel, I had the dollar bills ready for the outstretched hands I had neglected the first time around.

God placed His most important words in Scripture. We mentioned this in earlier chapters. God recently asked me to memorize the book of Mark. Now, all the time, I hear His words through Mark when I am trying to make a decision. How much of His Word do you have in your heart to help you in decision-making?

Listening hard does not always mean we will hear. Sometimes, our deafness is not our fault. We spoke earlier of the noise of life. We live in a world where the noise of life is often so loud that the whisper of God is muffled beyond recognition.

Not long ago I received a frantic text message from a physician friend in the Midwest. Our back and forth text messages over the next 30 minutes put blisters on my thumbs. The gist of the frantic and rambling discussion was that he was totally overwhelmed; he felt unappreciated and was losing his faith in the midst of it all. Knowing him as a brilliant young man with a solid work ethic, I was certain he was under tremendous time and work pressure. Some of my text reply included, "Ultimately God hears and loves us whether we feel it or not. I have no doubt you will connect with Him again. Right now, I think you need to find a way to cut out the least important thing you are doing and give yourself a little space to allow you to sort things out."

Sometimes, when we try to make decisions under intense pressure, the noise of life drowns out the whisper of God. In such times we need to remove ourselves from the noise. We need to let go of some squawking beast to which we have become attached or some pleasant song that draws us away from God.

What pleasant or discordant noise is drowning out God's whisper in your ear? What things of lesser importance can I release in order to focus on God's leading? Do I need to drop a responsibility that others can do well? Do I need to take time off and retreat into the silence so I may hear the King? The more important the decision, the more we need to remove the noises that dampen our hearing.

And so, our God often walks in shadows and often speaks in whispers, but when we hear Him and obey, life explodes with purpose and value.

Albert Schweitzer describes the whisper of God that exploded him out of success toward the poorest of the poor in the town of Lambaréné in Gabon, Africa: "You are happy...therefore, you have been called to give up more. Whatever you have received more than others in health, in talents, inability, in success...you must not take to yourself as a matter of course. You must pay a price for it."

He concluded his thoughts, "The voice is dangerous for the happy when they have the courage to listen for it...It challenges them in an attempt to lead them away from the natural road, and to... make them adventurers of self-sacrifice, of whom the world has too few."

I cannot be certain, but I suspect God remains somewhat hidden so we might seek Him hard. And within that hard seeking, hard looking, hard listening, we are changed. We develop trust and patience. We develop a determination to follow Him that only comes from nights of darkness. We hone our ears and sensitize our vision so we can find Him more often as we walk through each day—His servants in a world He is redeeming. It is likely that our ability to hear Him speak to us throughout our day is more important than the one word we are seeking for our present decision. When we train ourselves to listen hard, He builds us into the kind of people who can recognize His voice, even when He whispers. And, when we hear His whisper, He breathes the possibility of redemption and eternity into the common decisions we face each day we live.

Next Steps

1. Each morning for one week, ask God to show Himself to you in any way He wishes.
2. Each evening for one week, look back and list the ways you have seen Him or heard Him speak. You can add extra sheets.
3. Choose a significant chapter of Scripture and memorize it over the next two months.

Watch how it then informs your decision-making.

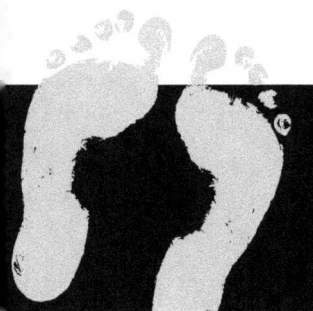

*Dear God,
Help me to become sensitive to your voice and presence in my daily life.
Amen*

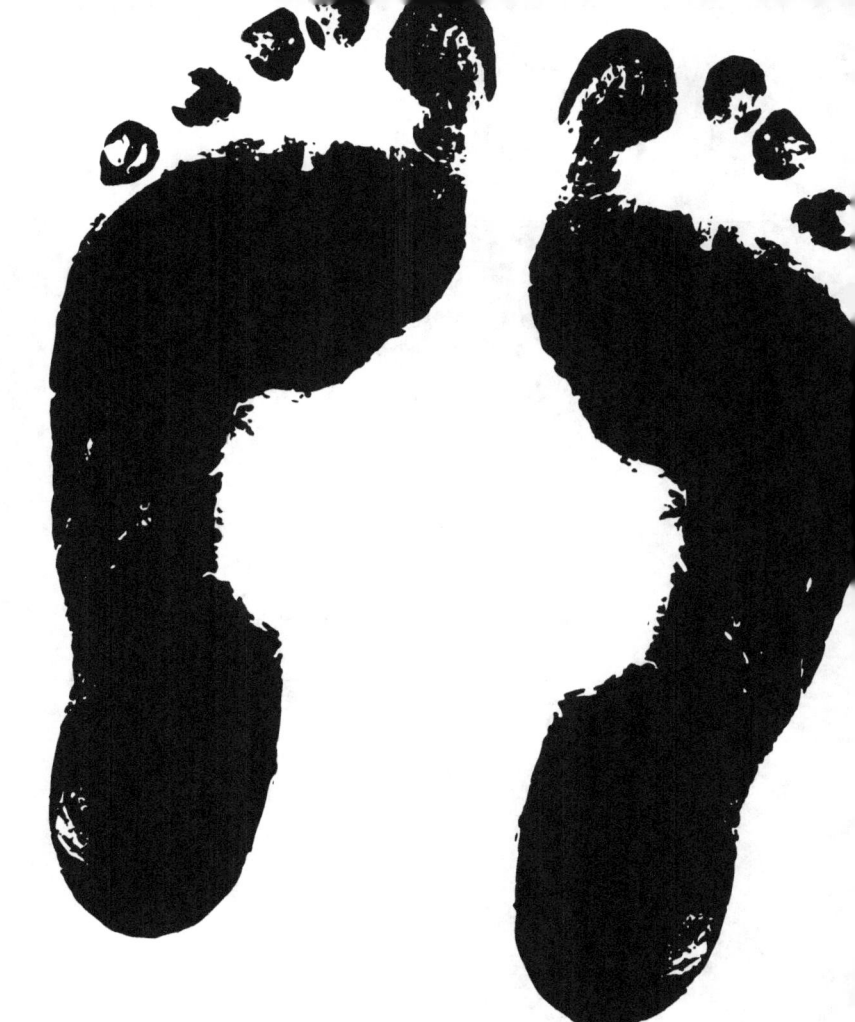

Step Nine
Obedience

> "The man who says, 'I know him,' but does not do what he commands is a liar, and the truth is not in him."
>
> —1 John 2:4
>
> ---
>
> "Only he who sees obeys, and only he who obeys sees."
>
> —Dietrich Bonhoeffer

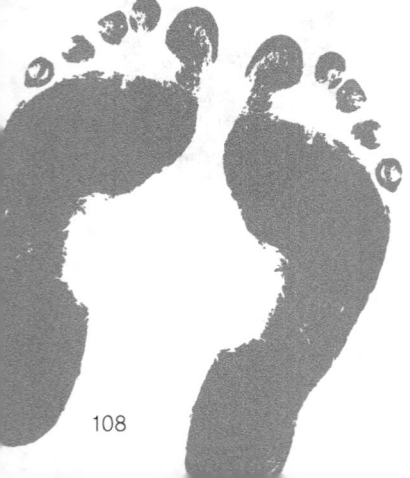

Step Nine
Obedience

I love to listen to answering machines when I call to relay patient lab results that turn out fine. Some messages are fun, and some are challenging. Not so long ago, I called a man to let him know his CT scan was fine, and I heard the recorded message, "This is the day that the Lord has made; I will rejoice and be glad in it." Beautiful words, great reminder, and then the message continued, "This is the day that the Lord has made. Are you rejoicing?" A beautiful statement and then a challenge to live up to it.

The truth is: every statement the Lord makes in His Word is not just information for me to chew on. When the Lord speaks to us through His Scripture or His pastor or a sister in Christ, God demands a response, just like that answering machine.

Many of us spend time seeking to learn of God through reading or listening to great speakers. We gain warm or energetic feelings when we see what God has done in other lives. But all this feeling is wasted unless we take those words from God and direct them to ourselves as a challenge, "So now, what are you going to do about it?"

Each time I hear God speak to me through His Spirit, I should be asking, "What do you want me to do with this, Lord?"

This is especially true when I am seeking God's direction in my life.

Dietrich Bonhoeffer wrote in his great work *The Cost of Discipleship*, "Only he who sees obeys, and only he who obeys sees." Somehow, it is in our act of obedience that God most clearly shows Himself.

Oswald Chambers put it this way, "Obedience is the basis of Christian thinking. Never be surprised if there are whole areas of thinking that are not clear, and never will be until you obey."

He also wrote: "The wish ought to be followed by immediate obedience...It is better to never have seen the light, better never to wish to be what you are not than to have the desire awakened and never to have resolved it into action...It is better never to have had the light than to refuse to obey it."

These great servants of Christ are telling us that finding direction for a future decision is dependent on our obedience to God in the decisions presently before us. God placed a dynamic feedback loop within our lives. When God makes Himself known, we respond in obedience. With this obedience, God steps into our lives in a fresh new way, which builds our faith and allows us to see Him more clearly the next time He steps into our lives. Each step of obedience produces a greater clarity of vision.

Matthew came to our hospital as sick as anyone I had seen in Eku, Nigeria. He was wasted and febrile and severely anemic. His face was plastered to the bones like the pictures from Auschwitz or Dachau. His eyes had the blank stare of one looking into the next world. We treated him with anti-malarial medicines and broad-spectrum antibiotics, but we knew he would not make it without a blood transfusion. Blood was hard to come by in Eku, unless you had money or a relative to donate, and Matthew had neither. Jackie Legg, a missionary nurse, was happy to give one, but two were badly needed. Finally, a male nursing student offered to donate a unit, but only if we gave him a dozen eggs to renew his strength. His rationale was not sound, but he was rigid in his demand. The only eggs at that time on our entire missionary compound were my family's last dozen that we needed to feed our two small children, with no likely source of eggs for a long time. The Lord told my wife Becky to give the eggs. She obeyed. Matthew got his blood, survived and, over a long recovery period in the hospital, came to know Jesus as His Savior.

One week after we donated our eggs for Matthew, I was asked to speak at Pastor Ekhator's church in Benin City. His wife Catherine had been my patient. I attended the service and was invited to his home for lunch after church. They knew nothing of Matthew or the eggs. As I was leaving their home to drive back to Eku, Catherine held me up and said, "Wait, I have something for you." She came from the house with a bag that she put on my front seat. I thanked her as I opened the bag and found two and a half dozen eggs.

The importance of this story is not that God always pays us back more than we give; though He does, often in a different currency. The importance of the story is that Becky obeyed, and because she obeyed, God showed Himself to her in ways she would never have seen had she not. Her faith in God for the future is now strengthened by that "new song," that batch of eggs from a pastor's wife in Nigeria. And her clarity of vision has improved. She can now see God working and can hear Him calling more clearly than before. When she is seeking His direction for decision-making in the future, God's whisper will be louder than before. This is the positive feedback loop of obedience and faith: God leads to faith; faith leads to obedience; obedience leads to sight; sight leads to greater faith; greater faith leads to greater obedience; greater obedience leads to greater sight, etc., etc., etc.

Obedience Requires Change

Obedience does not come naturally. It often has to be carved into us by time, prayer, tears and circumstance. We are not always ready to obey when we begin our searches.

When our son was graduating from high school, we soon would become empty nesters. Finally, the time was coming when we could let go of our normal life responsibilities and serve God in a more complete way with our lives.

When could we get started? What would He have us do? How could we make it work with all of our ties to the normal life? Which direction would God take us? If our retirement income was not enough, should we wait awhile?

My wife and I probed the darkness, asking God to answer our questions so we could fulfill His call. Every probe came back empty...until we had become different people, until we were obedient and had let go of precious dreams we had held closely, until we were willing to obey God, no matter what—and then God flung the door wide open to our next adventure for Him. We ended that process of searching for God's will as different people from the ones who had started the search. And, as different people, we were ready to obey.

Obedience Requires Risk

Too often, we are not quite ready to obey when we begin to seek God's will. Many of us face important decisions in our lives and we listen hard to hear God's whisper. When it comes, we think we are ready to follow Him wherever He leads; and then we begin to ask our questions. Before we follow, we usually want to know how we can work it all out, so we can do it well for God (and minimize the damage to ourselves). We want certainty in our reasoning minds of the outcomes before we are willing to follow through.

But, usually, God's questions are not answered with intellect only. Usually, God's questions require action before all questions are answered. Very often we will not see the next step until we obey with the step He has already shown us.

Obedience takes courage, because obedience without full knowledge of the outcomes requires risk.

In his book The Insanity of God, *Nik Ripken shares the story of a Russian pastor sent to a Siberian prison because of his faith. His wife and children followed him there to support him in his suffering, and they too suffered. One night, the wife and three children ate their last bread and rested in the knowledge that they were about to starve to death if God did not provide. That same winter night God spoke to a church deacon 30 kilometers away and told him to get out of bed, hitch his horse to a sled and carry food to the starving family. The deacon, with good reason, argued with God that it was too cold and too dangerous. God continued to command him to go. The deacon then exclaimed that there were wolves out there that could eat his horse and then eat him as well. "I'll never make it back!" he cried out. God's Spirit then spoke to him clearly, "You don't have to come back. You just have to go."*

We as human beings are geared to evaluate risk/benefit ratios. By weighing the risk against the benefit, we come up with decisions that produce the best chance of gain and the least chance of pain. "God asked me to do this with Him. What will the consequences be? How much is the cost? What will it do to my business, my income, my relationships, my reputation and my family? I know where God is pointing, but I hesitate. I must be certain the benefit is worth the risk. *What if I never make it back?*" Our problem comes as we quantify risks and benefits with human eyes.

The truth of life tells us that the benefit of our actions for God may not be better health or better wealth or happier kids; the benefit of our actions for God is the presence and blessing of God for ourselves, the redemption of the world for others and the glory of God for Himself. The truth of life tells us that the risk of our actions for God may truly involve personal loss in the world, but that loss can never be final. Again, as my pastor often says, "The worst thing that happens to you will never be the last thing that happens to you. The last thing that happens to you will be Jesus." All loss will be redeemed; all ashes will become beauty; all broken hearts will be mended; the dead will rise; justice will come; God wins; we win. So, when you calculate the risk/benefit ratio of obedience based on the truth of life, the risk is always transient and the benefit always eternal.

If We Don't Obey, God Will Get Our Attention
Sometimes we think, "I'll just slide this one by the Lord." When we truly love Him, God just doesn't go away that quietly.

Dennis is a neurologist in the Northwest with numb feet. About 15 years ago, he was in Hawaii, body surfing with boogey boards. He was using one of his kid's broken boards. Coming in on a big wave, he nailed the beach with his head, pinching his cord against his spine. Under water he realized, "I'm paralyzed." He was an avid swimmer and, without panic, waited for his body to float to the surface where a wave flipped him onto his back. There he could breathe and call for help. His son thought he was joking. Three days later Dennis was able to walk with assistance. He experienced excruciating pain in the hands and arms, and it took two months for them to recover. He still walks carefully because of persistent loss of sensation in his feet. I asked him what he learned through that struggle. "Well, God sure got my attention," he said. I asked him what God had said to him and he answered, "God asked me, 'Who are you living for—you or me?'"

As C.S. Lewis describes from his own life experiences, "God whispers to us in our pleasures, speaks in our consciences, but shouts in our pains. It is his megaphone to rouse a deaf world." When Dennis now remembers his arm pain and near paralysis, he hears God's Spirit shouting out the suffering of Christ and is driven back to gratitude and service.

Obedience is Not Magic

A cautionary note must be mentioned regarding obedience. We obey because we love God, and we see Him step into our lives when we obey, but obedience is not a currency we can use to make God give us what we want.

Joseph is a vigorous and sweet 80-year-old widower I have cared for over the last five years. I was asking him about his diet recently—whether he was able to get vegetables to eat since he quit building a garden this year. He replied, "You know, there are these people who own a restaurant near me who cook the best vegetables. When they heard I was sick, they told me to come over anytime I wanted, and they would fix me whatever I want. I eat there nearly every day. I love their cabbage. They don't cook the ham hocks in it but got them separate, if you want to add them. And they have never charged me a dime. They tell me, 'Your money's no good here.'"

Sometimes I think my money's good with God, that my obedience might buy something I want from God. When bad things happen, I haven't paid enough; and when things go my way, it's because I'm all paid up. I forget the message of the cross.

It's all about grace. "While we were still sinners, Christ died for us" (Romans 5:8b). I don't know why my head can accept this truth but my heart keeps going back to my getting what I deserve. I guess it's because grace just doesn't seem fair.

Thank God He is not fair. Thank God "my money is no good with Him."

I am totally forgiven by His death on the cross, in spite of all my disobedience. And the converse is true: I should never think that God owes me my desires because in a few instances I actually obeyed. Obedience will open our ears to His whispers and allow us to hear more clearly His direction for our lives, but that direction will not necessarily bring us our personal dreams. Our dreams are not the issue here.

Are we willing to obey if God does make clear His answer to our questions? Are we willing to travel whatever path He will ask us to travel? Are we presently obedient in each direction He has already made clear? Is God worth the risk? God's willingness to make our decision clear may be dependent on our answers to these questions.

Next Steps

List one step you know the Lord would have you take, either directly related to your decision, or even unrelated. After you have done that, list a second step.

1. _____

   _____

2. _____

   _____

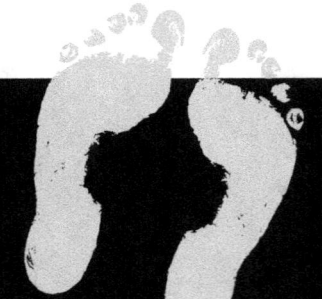

Dear Father,
Let me be faithful in that which you have already shown me and then let me see you in a new way.
Amen

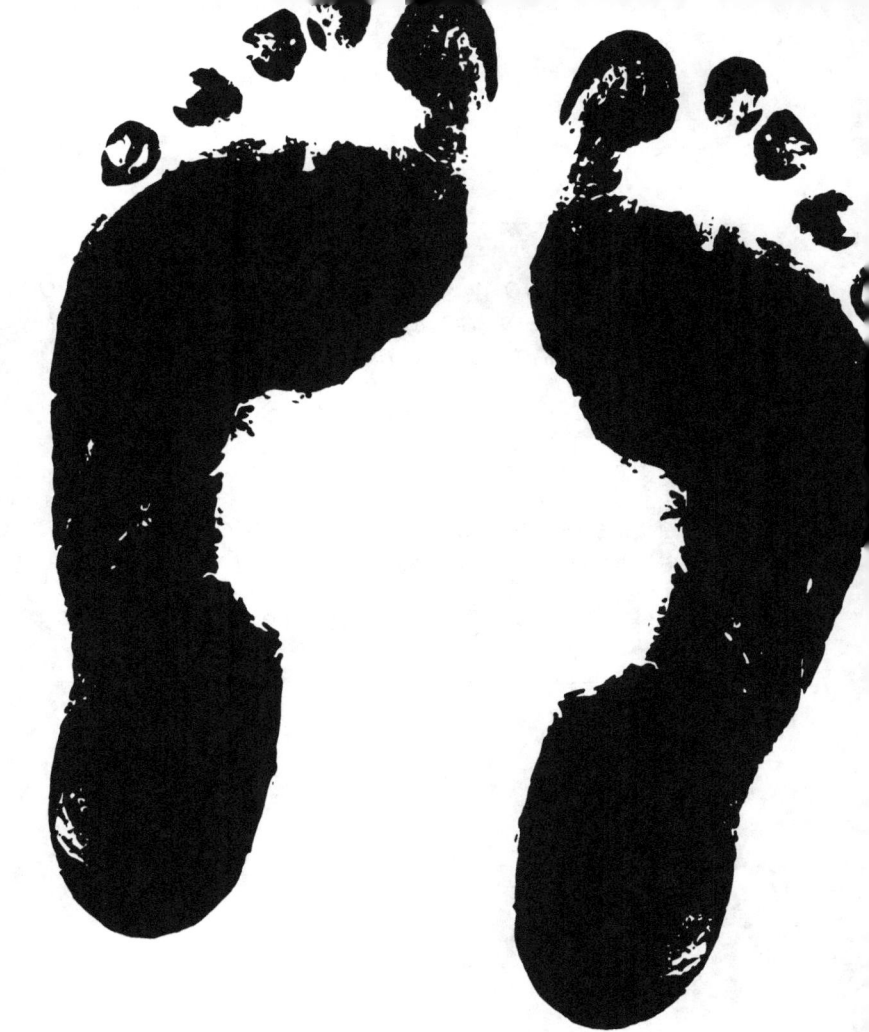

Step Ten
Trust

> "Trust in the Lord with all your heart and lean not on your own understanding; in all your ways acknowledge him, and he will make your paths straight."
>
> —Proverbs 3:5-6
>
> ---
>
> "To take the first step in faith, you don't have to see the whole staircase; just take the first step."
>
> —Martin Luther King

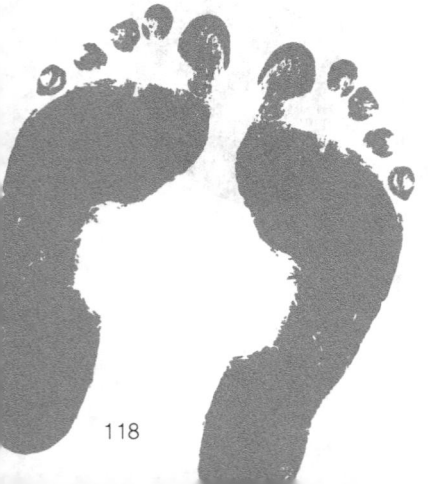

Step Ten
Trust

God speaks when we truly seek Him, when we listen hard for His whisper and when we are living a life of obedience. But, as I look at my own life's history, I'm stuck with the memories of the times God has spoken to me and I have not obeyed.

Why is that?

In my own life, most often, my lack of obedience comes from my lack of trust. I'm afraid I will lose if I obey, or afraid that God cannot, or will not, give me what I want if I obey.

Donald Hankey said, "True religion is betting one's life there is a God."

Am I willing to bet my life with my next decision that there is a God?

In her important work *Believing God*, Beth Moore nails my problem on the head. She reminds us that believing God is believing that:

"God is who he says he is." and
"He will do what he says he will do."

And then she summarizes my area of difficulty: "As Christians, we have no trouble believing in God; we have trouble believing the God we believe in."

That's where I am in much of my decision-making.

When we make a decision, are we banking everything on the truth of life that there is a God?

When we make a decision, do we believe the God we believe in?

C.T. Studd spent his life as a missionary in China and the Congo. Near the end of Studd's life, African believers themselves began to hear God's call to become missionaries among distant tribes. One such man was Zamu, a small man with a chronic foot injury. When Zamu was about to leave on his journey, the local Caucasian missionary was doubtful of his ability to survive.

"What about your foot, Zamu?"

"God is, White Lady."

"But the food is so different, down there—no palm oil or salt."

"God is, White Lady."

"You might starve or be killed."

"God is."

"What about your wife?"

"She will accompany me, White Lady. God is."

(from C.T. Studd: Cricketer & Pioneer *by Norman Grubb)*

God is.

I'm old enough that I prefer to pack my faith in little nutshells, so I can remind myself readily what life is all about. Such a nutshell is the brief statement from this crippled man of faith as I face my own questions and trials: God is.

What about life's tragedies? —God is.

What if I fail in my dreams for life? —God is.

What if I fail in God's mission for my life? —God is.

What about my children? —God is.

What about my finances? —God is.

What about my sin? —God is.

What about my death? —God is.

What about the outcomes of this decision? —God is.

There are few questions in life that cannot be answered victoriously by these two words. There are few decisions we need to make as Christians that can be made correctly without these two words.

In what ways can we trust the "God who is" as we seek the right answers for our decisions?

1. Trust that He will show us all that is necessary to get us on the right path.

Most of the correct decisions in my life have come from the factors we have already listed: abiding in Christ, walking in His presence, remaining true to His Word, obtaining wise counsel, etc. By living such a life, the best I can, God has guided me most often without miraculous intervention, with reason and conscience and "nudges" from His Spirit. But there have been a few occasions, of which I am not proud, when I was unable to follow His guidance because of my own sin and my desire to control the outcomes of my decisions. In those times, God did what was necessary to set me on the right path.

After God made it clear to us that He wanted us to serve Him in Nigeria, we went through a long process of preparation. I continued to work as a physician during that time with a private practice in internal medicine. As time wore on, I began to focus on the hardships I was about to place on my wife and 5-year-old daughter. Instead of focusing on Christ, I was focused on the difficulties ahead in a strange land. One morning in the shower I was overwhelmed with a sense of gloom over my family's future. My body was bathed half in shower water and half in tears. I broke. I told God I could not go through with the mission He had handed me, but I would give Him one chance to re-convince me.

I had a full medical practice and was not looking to sell it, but I wanted a Christian physician to take it over. I had no takers at the time. There was a particular young doctor I wanted to care for my patients, and I had approached him many weeks before but had heard nothing. So, I gave God this one chance, "If you have Dennis come to me this day and offer to take my practice, I will know for sure that I must go." This came not as a challenge, but as a cry of desperation and weakness.

That evening, I finished my practice at about 7 p.m. and was headed home when I got a call from the emergency room. I groaned and turned around. There was a back door, non-public entrance that I entered to find my patient. As I opened that door, in the distance I saw Dennis, whose name I had prayed that morning, and was immediately filled with an overwhelming sense of fear. Planning at all costs to avoid him (not out of disrespect for God, but out of pure fear of God), I snuck around the back halls to find my patient and care for her. As I was writing my note at the physician's substation in that back hall, I felt a tap on my shoulder. It was Dennis asking if I still wanted him to take my practice. Wham!

This was not a pleasant experience, but it was a convincing one. I understood then the Jewish proverb that states, "God is not a kindly uncle; He is an earthquake." As far as I can remember, I have never again asked God for such a specific sign. I am surprised He did not just give up on me in that shower. God did not reveal Himself in this magnificent manner because I was a man of great faith, but because I was a man of little faith. A man or woman of great faith would not have needed such a sign. Yet, my very meager faith was enough for Him to use in an extraordinary way to set me on the right path. I was a man who wanted God's will first, and He did what was necessary to show me.

I experienced another such divine encounter on the other end of my foreign mission experience.

After two years in Africa, my wife became ill and we were faced with the decision of leaving the mission field and coming home. This was as heartbreaking a decision as the shower event three years before. We spent months in prayer, in Christian counsel, with good medical advice, and still there was no clear direction from God. Becky and I were sitting in the side yard under our almond tree, where our 2-year-old daughter had spent her rainy seasons playing naked in the rain. There was a half-moon in the sky and Becky was crying in her garden chair. Hundreds of lightning bugs lit up the grass. I still could not bring myself to say out loud, "It is God's will that we go home," but I thought He was leading us that way. I was praying sincerely, and I felt the presence of God. Looking up to palm leaves blowing in the breeze, I saw, suspended in air, a blonde-haired girl moving toward me with a strong wind blowing her, almost on her side, leaves swirling around her. She continued toward me and then stopped as the wind ceased. I then imagined or heard her voice saying, "Take her home." And I did.

Again, I am not proud of either moment of God's extraordinary revelation. I have not had another in the 30 years since. Both were moments of weakness for me. But I praise God He was willing to speak to me in the language I needed at the time. Praise God He is willing to meet us wherever we are if we are truly seeking His will; and praise Him that He is willing to do whatever is necessary to place us on His path when our hearts are set on Him. Most of the great decisions in my life have not required extraordinary revelation but have come with a simple, settled understanding after examining the circumstances in prayer: my choice of profession, asking my wife to marry me and even the initial call into missions. But God will do what it takes. I firmly believe that if we seek and desire His path with all our hearts, He will place us on it—usually without the theatrics I required in these two instances, but whatever it takes.

2. Trust enough to take the first step.

Mother Teresa did not begin her life as a Nobel Laureate and Saint, though that is who she became. She began her life as Gonxha Agnes Bojaxhiu, an Albanian girl born in Skopje, Macedonia. She grew up loving Jesus and gave her life to him to serve as a missionary when she was 12 years old. She had no idea how God's plan would develop. At the age of 18 she decided to become a nun and wrote a letter to the superior of the Loreto nuns. The letter ended:

"I don't have any special conditions, I only want to be in missions, and for everything else I surrender myself completely to the good God's disposal." (From Mother Teresa: Come Be My Light. The Private Writings of the Saint of Calcutta *by Mother Teresa)*

She did not know where that first step would lead, but by taking it, Mother Teresa became the greatest model for Christ's love in the 20th century. It was her step into a world where she had no expectations of her future, "I don't have any special conditions," surrendering "completely to the good God's disposal."

When God does speak, it is often into a world where only the first step is seen. Sometimes we "place our fingers in our ears," like my sweet granddaughter did in the introduction of this book, and refuse to listen because we cannot see the steps beyond the first. We are afraid that once we have committed, the rest may be too much for us; and so, we close our ears to protect us from the command.

Martin Luther King, Jr. knew what it was to step into a dangerous future where there was only uncertainty: "To take the first step in faith, you don't have to see the whole staircase; just take the first step."

His step in Selma changed all of history.

That first step is often the step of obedience that God requires for us to prove our faith and to grow our faith. God then takes that step of faith and uses it as a switch to turn on the light and ignite the power of His plan.

Can we take the one step we see clearly and trust God with the rest? If we cannot, we are covering our ears; and the voice of God, that we so much want to hear for direction, will grow harder and harder to distinguish from the sounds of the world.

Again, from Oswald Chambers: "Obedience is the basis of Christian thinking. Never be surprised if there are whole areas of thinking that are not clear, and never will be until you obey."

3. Trust God with wrong turns.
So, we hear God speak and we take the only step we know; and, just as we feared, things turn out badly. Did we hear God wrong? Were we foolish to think we could hear Him at all? Such thoughts often flow through our brains as we try to discern whether it is really God speaking to us or just our imagination. Such thoughts make it difficult to trust enough to take that next step we need in order to find the third.

One of the truly freeing discoveries I have made in Christian decision-making is that we can trust God even if we make the wrong decision, as long as that decision was based on a desire to seek His will above our own. It is our job to seek His will with all our heart and to take that first step. It is totally God's problem to make that step work out. If we desire His will and follow it to the best of our understanding, but make a mistake in discerning His will, it is God's business to fix it and place us back on the path He prefers.

I learned this best from a broken brush.

We had been back from Nigeria for 18 years, and I had spent most of that time in private practice. My son was graduating from high school this year. We would be empty nesters and I could hear God calling. Once again, I had the possibility of returning to the mission field—back to Africa. I prayed with my wife and we communicated with each other to the degree that I understood communication. We both knew God was calling us into a new adventure.

My eyes and heart were set on an opportunity in Cameroon. I could feel that this was the right direction. In order to move forward toward that opportunity, there was paperwork to be done. Mine was quickly completed, but I kept watching the dust gather on my wife's. Finally, one Sunday morning as we were getting ready for church, I walked into the bathroom where she was brushing her hair. I spoke softly, with great kindness, "You haven't filled out your application." I can see now in slow motion how she raised that plastic hairbrush above her head, then lowered it rapidly onto the bathroom sink with such force that the plastic shattered all over the bathroom. "You're not listening to me!' she shouted. "If God calls me to Africa, I will go to Africa; but God is not calling me to Africa." I took a deep breath, walked out of the room and checked Africa off my list. God had something better.

I had chosen the wrong step, and God turned me. Sometimes it is easy to hear what God is saying, and other times the world or our personal agendas drown out God's whisper. No problem. So He shouts it through your wife with plastic flying everywhere. God did not want us back in Africa; He had far better plans. I just needed Him to speak loudly enough to overcome the plans that were drumming away with my own tune of personal desire.

God is good like that. We might really want His will but, in spite of our good intentions, might start off heading in the wrong direction. Our faith should be strong enough to trust God to correct us if our good-intentioned way is wrong. If our hearts are right and we want His will more than our own, God will get us on the right path, whatever it takes. I'm just glad the brush hit the countertop and not my head.

4. Trust Him with the outcomes.

When I returned from the mission field as a young doctor, I was desperate to return to a life of service internationally. One day I was serving as a representative for our local group at Christian

Medical & Dental Associations' National Convention when I felt a tap on my shoulder: "I hear you want to do some volunteer mission?" The white-haired surgeon I met that day, Dr. Bill Johnson, was leading a Christian educational mission to Albania and told me the Albanian doctors had asked for an oncologist. I felt this was God's will, prepared the lectures, took the 10 days off and traveled with a team to Tirana, Albania. I had no idea what I was going to do when I arrived.

On the first day I was greeted casually by the oncology team and taken to tour their hospital. After a brief tour, they clearly told me they did not need me and had wanted a surgical oncologist, not a medical oncologist. Weeks of preparation, lots of personal money—and here I was, unwanted and unneeded by the people God had called me to serve.

In my state of rejection, I wandered across the hospital compound to the only other area of medicine in which I was qualified, hematology. With an interpreter I greeted the chief of hematology, Dr. Pal Xhumari, and told him I would be happy to help them in any way I could. I was not prepared for his anger. Others had come before me since Albania had opened up to the West. Others had promised, taken advantage of him and left without fulfilling their promises. Why should he think I was different?

Wow. A stranger in a strange land, only here to help a great medical need and to bear witness for Christ—I had taken that first step when God spoke and had landed in a pile of poo. It was apparent that I would fail in this mission on all counts. But I would not let go of God's possibilities. I told Dr. Xhumari that I could not speak for or defend those who had come before me. I told him I was in Albania and in his office for no other reason than to help him.

"Let's do this," I offered. "You make a list of supplies you need that are important to your work here. I will promise to do my best to return to Albania and bring you all I can."

Dr. Xhumari made the list. Six months later I returned with more than $250,000 worth of medicines and hematology equipment, totally by God's provision. And the hematology chief began to trust me. My relationship with Dr. Xhumari has now lasted 25 years, with my returning to his country regularly, with him and his wife staying in my home and studying in our hospital system twice, with six of his colleagues spending a month each in my home studying hematology, with an incredibly beautiful ministry for Christ developing among the Albanian medical, dental and nursing students over those years.

God spoke, and all I did was take the first step, the only step I could see; after that step, God did a wonderful thing, totally different than anything I could imagine. If I had I planned the outcomes of that first encounter, it would never have been as glorious as it has become. Our job is to desire and step. God gets all the credit and all the blame after that. If we only make decisions where we can predict and control the outcomes, we will rarely end up on the path God has planned for us. Our thoughts and plans are so much smaller than God's. God's plan is so much greater than ours; we must trust Him with all outcomes.

That's not always easy. God's outcomes at times may be quite painful, but they are the outcomes chosen by the Creator of the Universe, who proved His love for us on a cross.

I paraphrase John McMurray who said it best: "Do not be afraid. The things you fear may well come to pass, but they are no reason to be afraid."

We may face the outcome we most fear when following God's call, but we must trust that outcome to the only One who can make dry bones come to life (Ezekiel 37), the only One who can redeem all outcomes. God thinks on a huge, eternal scale, and He thinks with love. We must trust Him with the results of His plans.

It's important that we, at times, gain a glimpse of His big story, so we can trust God to place our little story within it.

Very often, the things we perceive as most important are not so important in God's great plan for us.

Charlie was a soft-spoken, Christian physician and friend of mine, whom many believed to be the best cardiovascular anesthesiologist around. Some time ago in his home, he rose to speak after many fellow physicians and church elders had completed an anointing service for his healing. Metastatic pancreatic cancer had found its way into his liver, and Charlie had started a journey he had not planned to travel for many years. His wife had spoken before Charlie's time to speak and declared, "We stand on the solid rock of Jesus Christ. We are praying for a miracle and I believe God will bring one. If not, we will still be okay." Charlie then stood and spoke briefly, "Thank you all for coming. We'll get through this, either way."

Charlie had a battle ahead but had already won. "The things you fear may well come to pass, but they are no reason to be afraid."

That night in his home was proof. As I sat on their stairway, I thought: when we as Christians look at our lives and really examine our deepest desires, these deepest desires are rarely transient and tied to health or longevity. Our greatest dreams are the stuff that eternity is made of. And Charlie, in spite of cancer, had already won his deepest desires.

To be loved: I saw the family and friends who gathered; Charlie had already won.

To make a difference in the lives of others: I've heard the testimonies of doctors, nurses, friends and family who have been blessed by Charlie's touch.

To care for our families: Each of us someday must "let go and let God" with our families. Charlie said that night, "I'm blessed to have the time to prepare things for my wife and daughter."

To leave a legacy: Enough folks have said enough things for me to know Charlie's influence in their lives will go on and on. I know his courage in this battle will change me forever.

To bring glory to God: Janice and Charlie continued to express their love for God no matter who was in the room.

To live: Under the blood of Christ, Charlie would never die. He's already won.

There are certainly lesser goals that we all seek in life. Charlie did too. He did not achieve them all during life on this side of the door. Lesser battles were lost, and those losses hurt deeply. But they were not the war. They were not the strategic victories that Charlie needed to make life worth it all. Those victories were already won.

Two important issues rise from Charlie's story as it relates to decision-making.

The first is this: God's scale of outcomes is far greater than ours, eternally greater. We must trust Him that He is fitting our present decision into His scale and into His big story, not just into our small scale and little story.

As Jim Elliot reminded us, "He is no fool who gives what he cannot keep to gain what he cannot lose."

The second lesson from Charlie's story is this: "Either way." If we cannot say to God with our present decision, "Either way," God may not think it helpful to clarify for us which way is His.

I mentioned earlier Tom Blumer, a friend of mine who died recently. He was a true man of God. Throughout his illness—with the discovery of his cancer, the initial surgeries and chemotherapy, the recurrence, the advanced surgery and treatment, the word that he was going to die from his illness—he was a man of faith.

At the funeral, Jerry, a fellow church member, told the story of telling Tom about a friend of his who also had cancer. Tom asked Jerry, "Do you mind if I call him?" Tom did and struck up an ongoing conversation that lasted until Jerry's friend died three weeks before Tom. At the funeral, Jerry told us, "My friend was not a Christian before, but I am confident I will see him in heaven, because Tom used the rest of his life to talk to my friend about Jesus."

The strongest kind of faith. One that reaches outward, as well as inward.

Many of us have faith that God is with us in our circumstances.

We have faith that God will help us with our needs.

We have faith that heaven is out there for us someday.

We have faith that God will care for those we love.

Each of these areas of trust in our lives is real and important.

But each has ourselves as the beneficiary.

The strongest faith lets go of our benefit and seeks God's will alone.

5. Trust with His mission.
For some of us the most difficult thing to trust to God is the ministry He has handed us for His glory. We have taken that mission faithfully and nurtured it. Now we have a decision to make which might endanger that for which we have worked so hard. As this decision lies before us, we first have to decide, "Can I trust God with this ministry if He leads me to a decision that might diminish its effectiveness or even survival?"

We hold to the ministry as if it were ours and not His. We refuse to consider a decision that might harm the ministry we love.

> *In his book* Ruthless Trust, *Brennan Manning tells the story of the last days of his dear friend, Dominique Voillaume. Near the end of Dominique's life, when he had developed the cancer that would take him to heaven, he retired from the Catholic priesthood and moved to Paris, where he took a job as a night watchman. Each morning as his shift ended, he would visit the*

park across the street from his house, where lived the homeless, alcoholic, drug abuser, worthless in the eyes of the city. He would pass out candy, listen to their stories and tell them that Jesus loved them. Dominique died. The final entry in his diary shouts at my desire to protect my mission for God from God. He wrote: "All that is not the love of God has no meaning for me. I can truthfully say I have no interest in anything but the love of God, which is in Christ Jesus. If God wants to, my life will be useful through my words and witness. If He wants to, my life will bear fruit through my prayers and sacrifices. But the usefulness of my life is His concern, not mine. It would be indecent of me to worry about that."

Am I worried I will make a decision that will harm God's kingdom, or am I more worried that I will make a decision that will harm my value as His servant?

"The usefulness of my life is His concern, not mine. It would be indecent of me to worry about that."

God brought this lesson home to me recently when we were planning our next mission trip to Albania.

For more than 20 years God had been sending us to Albania on Christian educational ministry to the medical and dental community of Tirana. Over the years this ministry evolved into an intense focus on medical students with a strong Christian student leadership core. We were now letting them direct the ministry, with us as resource providers for doctors and funding. Two of us from America had been the leaders and primary speakers for the symposiums we held each year, a mixture of both clinical and evangelical emphases. Last spring the Albanian student leadership asked us to dramatically expand our ministry to include nursing and pharmacy. We followed through with that request and were leading a large team including nurse educators—until three weeks before departure, when the students told us that surprise exams had been scheduled and the medical personnel were no longer needed. Tickets purchased, coverage for home accomplished. "We don't need you...but we do want your nurses." Slapped hard by the news, we sent the nursing team with untested leadership and I stayed home. The mission trip proceeded with a number of leadership and emergency complications but ended successfully.

Two weeks later I received an email report regarding the trip in which I, the leader, was unable to attend. The student leader posted, "God is great. This was the best mission to our students that we have ever completed!" The best ever—my mission, without me.

This experience has let me take to heart a lesson I had known in mind only: No mission for God is mine. They are all His. No mission for God depends on me. They only depend on Him. Therefore, when I make decisions in the future, because God has brought this lesson home to me, I will be able to hear and accept God more clearly when He says, "This plan doesn't include you."

God will not lead us down a path that will thwart His plan to redeem the world, even if the path He chooses will diminish the ministry He handed to us. Am I willing to hear this message, should God whisper it in my ear? Or is my pride shouting so loudly that I am unable to hear His whisper?

My friend Charles Ray described it best:

"Last summer I was walking along a bay in Louisiana near where large vessels were going out to sea. The constant churning of water from their wake pushed the froth up against the beach, mixed with the oil from their engines. The oil had infiltrated the froth and produced large bubbles. Because of the oil, the bubbles reflected light in radiant colors. They looked like brilliant jewels at the water's edge. The oil produced a cohesiveness that allowed me to actually pick up the bubbles without breaking them and I was able to hold these beautiful jewels in my hands. When I was finished with the beauty of each, I tossed it back into the bay. My service to God has been like one of those waterside jewels. Not to be kept and held, but

to beautifully serve the plan that God has for that moment and then to be released without ownership or even retrievability."

6. Trust Him with those we love.

Will we listen to Him and trust God when it affects not just ourselves but also those we love most? Will our concern for our loved ones drown out His whisper into our decisions?

When we come to Jesus for decisions, we do not come with our arms at our sides or even our arms raised up in praise; instead, we come with our arms wrapped around those we love and those for whom we are responsible. There is no greater responsibility on earth for us than to care for our families. Are we willing to listen to God if His answer may place their happiness or safety at risk? Not always.

As Oswald Chambers reminds us, "The thing that hinders God's work [most] is not sin, but other things that are right, but which at a certain point in their rightness conflict with the claims of Christ."

It has only been a few years since I told God to let go of my daughter. My older daughter has had a very unhappy life related to her bipolar illness. She has suffered greatly in abusive relationships and addictions; and yet, she is a daughter I love with all my heart. I have prayed consistently with tears over her life of sadness, ultimately giving her to the Lord for His best plan, trying my best to make decisions around her life that were God-led and not Daddy-led. I decided to take my hands off her life and let God do His will with her. A few years ago, she went through another time of great suffering when she lost someone she loved. Her life spiraled down into terrible agony. I had had enough.

"You can't have her anymore!" I shouted to God. "You have made a mess of it, doing it your way, and I am done with that. I am taking her back and making the decisions I think will most make her happy."

That rebellion only lasted a few months before I handed her back to the Father who created and loved her far more than I. But I understand the pain of fathers who must make decisions, led by God, which could cause great pain to those they love. Somehow, we must hand them over to the One who loves them far more than we.

Charles Ray Griffin is a hero in my life. When I was in college, he was the one who taught me how to pray. I still see him from time to time. Recently on a visit he told me a story: "You know you made me very mad once," he chuckled. "It was a Sunday when you were the assigned deacon to visit the church visitors. This was a time in my life where I had very little time at home, due to work, to raise my children in the Lord. My wife was less avid about it than I. I was off work that Sunday afternoon and it was to be a precious day with them. And then you came up and asked me to join you in visitation. The assistant pastor heard you and gave me a special card with the name of a young man he wanted me to contact. I was furious. This was a day I was going to spend with my children and focus on their spiritual development. I made you do all the door visits while I stayed in the car and sulked. I missed my chance to spend time with my children. After we finished with your cards, we went to find the man on my card, but he was not home. Later that week I felt compelled by God to find the young man. I did. He was a college student I helped with a number of things, and then he disappeared from my life. For some time, I carried with me the resentment that I had so little time in those days to nurture my three children spiritually and I was deeply concerned for their salvation. One Sunday night I was in the back of the church praying as the service ended. I looked up during the invitational music and saw my son walking down the aisle to accept Jesus as his Savior. And, out of the corner of my eye, I saw another figure moving to the front of the church to stand beside my son. It was that college student whose card had made me so mad that day, the one whom God told me to go back and visit. He, too, was coming to declare Jesus as Lord."

Charles Ray and I talked over that story. We talked of listening for God, and of obeying God when He speaks, and of God's ability to best care for those we love when we most listen for and follow His will. Does this mean that making a decision that places our loved ones in harm's way will always be honored with their safety and happiness? Of course not, this is not the truth of life. In his book *The Insanity of God,* Nik Ripken speaks of the tragedy of death in his family as a result of his obedience to follow God to Africa. But, as we quoted before: "Do not be afraid. The things you fear may well come to pass, but they are no reason to be afraid."

In God's great eternal story of redemption and love, those we love are far safer when we listen and follow God's whisper than when we refuse to listen because of our fear.

How can we be really sure when God is calling us to making a decision where our families might suffer? We must be very careful. Sometimes we mess up. I mentioned earlier the young Christian couple whose family was torn apart and bankrupted because the husband became totally convinced God would have him give up his work and sacrifice the financial support his family needed to survive. The man left his wife and never accomplished his mission for God. Delusional or intense dedication? Of course, we can never be certain, but we should use all measures available for us to find God's will and continue to question any plan that hurts our family until God makes it very clear. It is especially important to listen to wise Christian counsel and to walk within biblical guidelines when faced with such decisions. Thank God His Spirit is alive and works with us as we move forward.

7. Trust that someday we will see.

Just as God may not lead us down ministry paths we might prefer, He often leads us down pathways that accomplish missions we are now unable to see. Abraham traveled his entire life without clearly seeing the mission accomplished. That's hard. All of us wish to see that our lives accomplished what God placed us here for. Many have lived a life of great disappointment, in spite of great service, because they have not realized God's victory through their faithfulness in this life. Hebrews 11:35-39 describes such lives of faith. These verses conclude with, "These were all commended for their faith, yet none of them received what had been promised." God's truth is, we will all someday see the results of God's work through our lives and receive the victor's crown.

Keith Giffin is my son's father-in-law and a long-time dentist in Mississippi. He tells the story from his Boy Scout days when he and his fellow scouts were riding in the back of a truck on a tortuous backwoods road. The driver of the truck was forced into a steep and sharp curve, jettisoning Keith and his buddy. Scraped up on the gravel road, they struggled to catch up with the truck and found another scout on the road, injured far worse than they. The poor young man had fallen beneath the back wheels. One leg was nearly torn off and the other crushed. Keith remembers vividly the boy's femoral artery, pointing upward in defiance, torn loose and pumping large steams of pulsatile blood everywhere. He also remembers reaching down and pinching the end of that artery for 25 minutes on the drive to Philadelphia, Mississippi where the boy was flown by helicopter to the closest major medical center in Jackson. Keith can still feel the cramp in his hand from the prolonged pressure on that artery. The boy never returned to school; however, Keith knew he had survived and lost his leg. Keith did not see the result of that long ride, so filled with effort and emotion, until the day he began dental school. Keith listened as they called out the names of his fellow classmates. The boy he saved was one of them.

Someday, guaranteed, we will discover that what we did in this life truly mattered.

We push so hard to make things happen: for our patients, our families, our jobs. And yet, we still come to those moments of reflection where we ask ourselves, "Did it really even matter?" All that pressure and hard work and sacrifice—we often don't see an outcome equal to the effort.

Even my work for Jesus. How many lives were really saved or fellow believers really nurtured or hungry really fed because I was faithful?

We work so hard to make life count, and yet there is so little we see to be counted. But God knows best. If we counted our successes, we would not handle the knowledge well. Like poor King David. At the very end of his life he wanted to measure all he had accomplished—how powerful was the kingdom God created through him? It didn't work out so well (2 Samuel 24).

I am totally convinced for my own life that God does not want me to measure the outcomes of His work through me, other than to see if I have been faithful. Everything else is way above my pay grade.

But I am also convinced that one day we will see it all. That one day God will set before us, not only our failures, but also all He accomplished when we followed Him faithfully—all of the pinched arteries that led to dental classmates—when we had no idea. And I think most of us will be gloriously surprised.

When we are facing important decisions in our lives, do we trust God with the outcomes? If we do not, our ability to hear His voice will never rise above the cacophony of our fear and our personal desires. But, if we lay it all in His hands and listen hard, regardless of our fears, we should be able to take the step that will place us on a pathway with Him beside us, with no obstacles possible to defeat His plan of love.

Next Steps

As you look forward toward your present decisions, list the one thing you trust God least with in stepping forward. Each morning until your decision is made, hand that one thing to Jesus.

1. _____

_____

_____

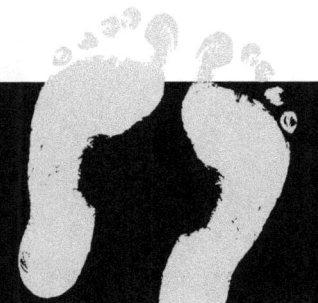

Dear Father,
I believe in you. Help me to believe you as well.
Amen

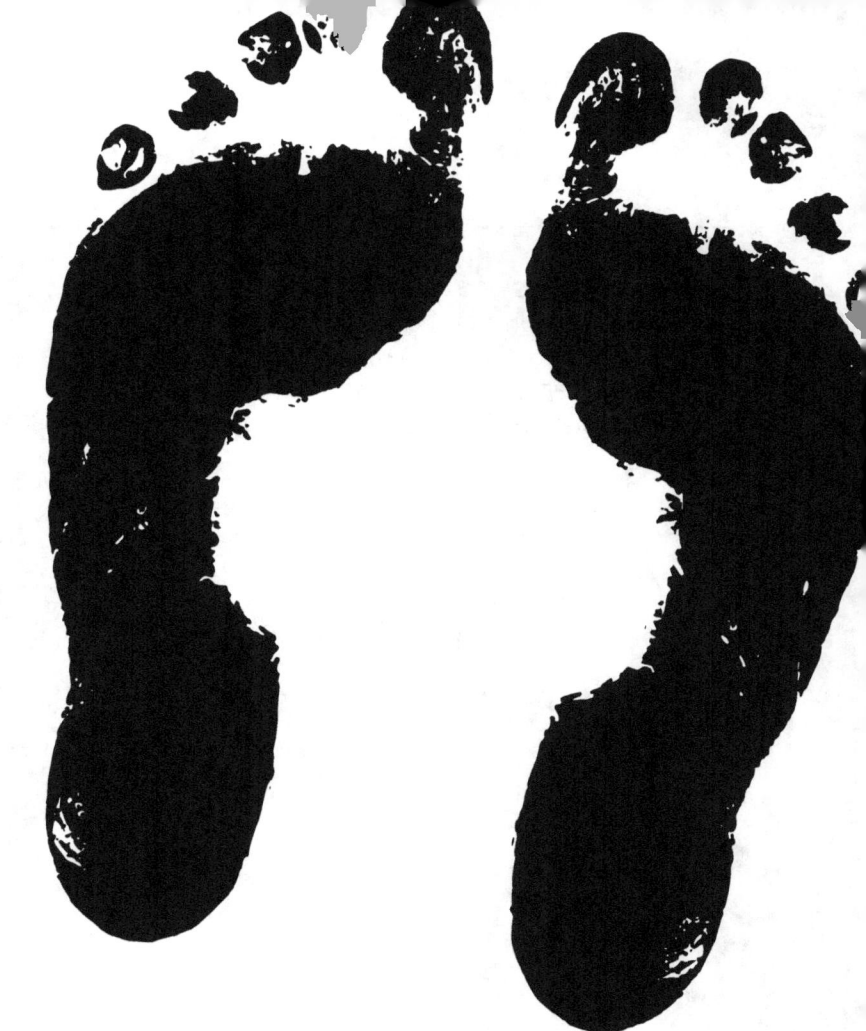

Step Eleven

Remove the Sin that Binds and Blinds

> "Therefore, since we are surrounded by such a great cloud of witnesses, let us throw off everything that hinders and the sin that so easily entangles, and let us run with perseverance the race marked out for us."
>
> —Hebrews 12:1
>
> ---
>
> "The essence of sin is my claim to my right to myself."
>
> —Oswald Chambers

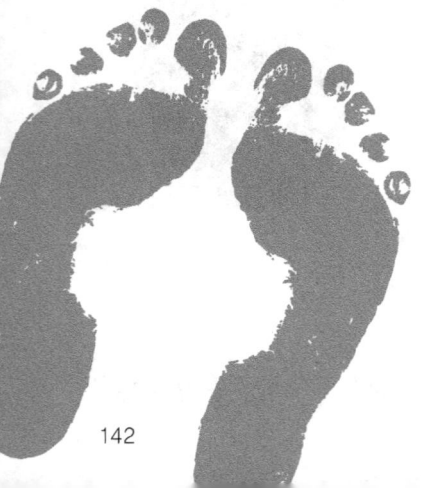

Step Eleven
Remove the Sin that Binds and Blinds

The story of Samson is both history and metaphor.

Samson was one of God's heroes. He lived in a time when most of the Promised Land was ruled by the Philistines, rather than by God's chosen people. Samson was a man dedicated to God, a Nazirite, who proved his special devotion by never cutting his hair. He chose for his wife a Philistine rather than an Israelite, against his father's wishes. This didn't turn out so well for her or for the Philistines; her people burned her up in a fire and Samson killed hundreds in revenge.

And then came Delilah. Samson fell in love, but Delilah was a spy. Samson first gave his heart to her and then handed to her the secret of his superhuman strength, his hair. While sleeping in her arms, Samson allowed Delilah to cut his hair. He awakened with Philistines pouring into the room, but his strength was gone. They bound him, blinded him and made him a public spectacle for all the Philistines to enjoy with laughter.

Samson had sinned. He had given his heart to a woman he cared for more than he cared for God, and eventually he handed her the blessing God had meant for His own glory. As a result, Samson was bound and could no longer see. God was able to redeem Samson, just as with the cross God redeems us all from any sin, but the binding and blinding remained (Judges 16).

There are times in our lives where we badly need God to help guide us in a decision. We truly desire His will in an area of our lives; we have gathered the facts; we have sought counsel; and yet, we are still unable to discern God's direction. If we find ourselves in such a place, we need to slip into a quiet closet and examine our lives to search for any sin that might be blinding us from seeing God's truth or binding us such that we are not willing to accept the light we see.

Sin is such a hard word to define, just as it is to talk about. We focus our understanding on the sin actions: kill, steal, lie, commit sexual immoralities, etc. But, as bad as they might be, the sin actions are but an outpouring of the real problem of who we are—sinners.

Watchmen Nee describes this understanding in his book *The Normal Christian Life*: "The teaching of Romans is not that we are sinners because we commit sins, but that we sin because we are sinners. We are sinners by constitution rather than action."

Oswald Chambers gives us the best definition of this state of sin nature: "The essence of sin is my claim to my right to myself."

Sin is choosing control over our own lives when God would have us hand our lives to Him. From such a choice all kinds of sin actions flow. Samson was a sinner who gave his heart to Delilah rather than God. This led to the action of handing over God's blessing of strength as well. We mimic this in our lives. Though saved from the penalty of sin in eternity, we as Christians continue to fight with the nature of sin that still wars within us on this side of glory. Sometimes this sin nature manifests itself in publicly decried sin actions like murder, adultery or cheating on business deals, even as Christians. Most of the time, the sin actions for Christ-followers are more subtle but just as dangerous.

When I attended my professional society meeting this year, I expected to gain some knowledge of science. I was surprised that I also gained some knowledge about myself. On the plane out, I sat across the aisle from a colleague in a more lucrative practice than mine who described the fun his expensive lifestyle provided. I thought, Oh, what I could do if I had his money. *On the convention shuttle, I sat next to a man, younger than I, who was prominent in his field. He spent the ride describing all his accomplishments and notoriety. I thought,* Oh, what I could do if I had his fame. *On the first meeting day, I received a call from my emotionally labile daughter—she had quit her job and was now unemployed. All my friends' children are successful professionals or missionaries. I thought,* Oh, what I could do if only my family were okay. *Too often I think,* Oh, what I could do if I were not who I am.

Envy is horrible. It comes from pride and self-focus, and it infects us all, even those who seem to have everything. Envy saps the joy from our lives. Envy damages my relationships with those I envy, relationships God has fashioned to complete His work of redemption. Envy was my sin.

And how is my sin of envy connected with decision-making?

How hard will it be for me to follow God's leading in a decision if I think it might diminish me in the eyes of others? How well might the shadow of envy hide the path that leads to more glory for Jesus but less for me?

There are many such acts of sin we need to watch out for in our lives, sins that may not make the newspapers. As C.S. Lewis describes in *Mere Christianity*: "The sins of the flesh are bad, but they are the least bad of all sins. All the worst pleasures are purely spiritual: the pleasure of putting other people in the wrong, of bossing and patronizing and spoiling sport, and back-biting, the pleasure of power, of hatred...that is why a cold, self-righteous prig who goes regularly to church may be far nearer to hell than a prostitute. But, of course, it is better to be neither."

The apostle Paul said nearly the same thing to Timothy: "People will be lovers of themselves, lovers of money, boastful, proud, abusive, disobedient to their parents, ungrateful, unholy, without love, unforgiving, slanderous, without self-control, brutal, not lovers of the good, treacherous, rash, conceited, lovers of pleasure rather than lovers of God—having a form of godliness but denying its power. Have nothing to do with them" (2 Timothy 3:2-5).

Which of these sins might be binding us, though they might never land us in prison? Which may be blinding us to God's direction?

Christian sin can be extremely subtle:

> *Dr. Mack was a new Christian in practice. He started out like most physicians, referring patients for consultation to those his partners recommended. Gradually his referral preferences drifted toward those who referred patients to him, realizing these physicians would reciprocate and help his doctor business grow. Then, one night his sister called him, asking for the best physician to perform a procedure for her. After he discussed the problem and made his recommendation, Dr. Mack realized that the best physician, to whom he had referred his sister, was not the one to whom he normally referred his patients. He had developed two standards of care: one that improved his referral base and one that was the best for his patients. Conflict of interest is a subtle beast built upon the foundations of pride and greed.*

Or, how about this one?

> *I was checking the vital signs of one of my patients from my home computer just prior to morning rounds this week. I saw her blood pressure had dropped to 77/45 and knew she was in trouble. So, I skipped breakfast and rushed to the hospital. This patient was admitted many months ago and I had been struggling to pull her through a complex disease. She was my only patient in this particular hospital and I had been seeing her daily for two months. As I got out of the car in the doctor's parking lot at 6 a.m. that morning, I began to think, "At least when she dies, I won't have to spend an extra 30 minutes coming here every morning."*

Have you ever had your "It's-All-About-Me" monster wake up when you least expect it? Even amid this great tragedy for a person I have loved and poured myself out for over two years, "It's-All-About-Me" woke up, pulled up a chair and took over the conversation. What is wrong with me?

I shouldn't be surprised; it's happened with my wife, my kids, my friends and my office staff. I'm not right—but I should know that from Scripture. I'm in good company. I am much like Paul, who did what he didn't want and couldn't do what he wanted (Romans 7:14-20).

Few would know this self-centeredness within me unless I told them, but God knows, and it muffles my communication with Him. Things He would like to tell me can't get through the muffle.

We are sinners. We live in a world where we are saved but still struggling with our old nature. We must accept this as fact if we are to deal with it and move toward overcoming.

> *I remember vividly a father and his son, standing against a wall printed with trees and streams—the dad in his blue scrub top, roughing his son's hair and then drawing him close for the picture. I watched them as I waited for my friend. I had promised to visit my friend in Pleasant Valley Prison and was angry with myself when the prison receptionist reminded me of the seven years since my last visit. They assigned us a table. My friend and I talked and laughed; and I watched the tears in his eyes for three and a half hours before he returned to his lifetime cell and I drove back to Fresno to catch a plane to a family I love. Lots of deep thoughts from that visit—but the picture that hangs most vividly in my brain is that father tussling his son's hair and then pulling him close against the artificial forest while his wife pointed the camera.*

There but for the grace of God go I.

Sometimes, as a physician, I walk proudly in my role. Sometimes, as a Christian, I feel good about myself.

But when I look at that father in prison blue, loving a son whom he could only pretend to really know, faced with a legacy not of pride but shame, I am humbled.

I know in truth that there is nothing that father did that I am not capable of doing, given the right motivation and the absence of God's protection. I am at my center a sinner, saved only by grace, empowered to live free from my sins only through the power of the One who lives within me. I make my rounds and sit in my church and hold my loved ones as a good man only because of the good in the One who died to break sin's grip on me.

Thank God for His grace. Thank God that we are slowly being delivered from the bonds of sin preventing us from having perfect communion with our Father while we live on this side of glory. But, we are sinners still and must recognize that our sin actions can prevent us from seeing God's beckoning hand and hearing God's whisper. We may act perfectly in all other aspects of seeking God's will, and yet, we fail to find His will because we do not let go of that which is more precious to us for the moment.

Our sin is blinding us to the direction God is providing.

So, how do we as Christians protect ourselves from our nature to sin? How do we as Christians protect ourselves from this subtle and nearly invisible serpent?

1. Be aware—we are vulnerable, and we are sinners.

2. Remember our covenant—we are saved by grace into a covenant whereby we have committed to following His will.

3. Be vigilant—we periodically need to reevaluate our lives to discover where the enemy has infected us.

4. Be accountable—if there are any areas of gray, seek counsel. Discuss it with trusted Christian friends and pastors.

5. Be determined—let the sin go, drive it from our lives, trusting in God's power to do so.

Often, it is only when we are delivered from our present sin that we can "take our sunglasses off in a dark room" and see the hand of God pointing us to His path, a path that leads to success, as He defines it, and to the glory we will all see someday.

Next Steps

List the areas in your life where sin is in charge rather than the Lord. Choose one sin action you will work with God to abandon.

1. _____
2. _____
3. _____
4. _____
5. _____

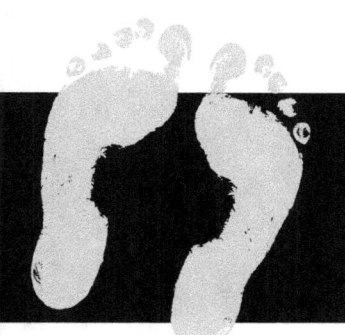

Dear Father,
Thank you for the cross that frees me from this sin blinding me to your will. I give this sin to you. In your power take it away.
Amen

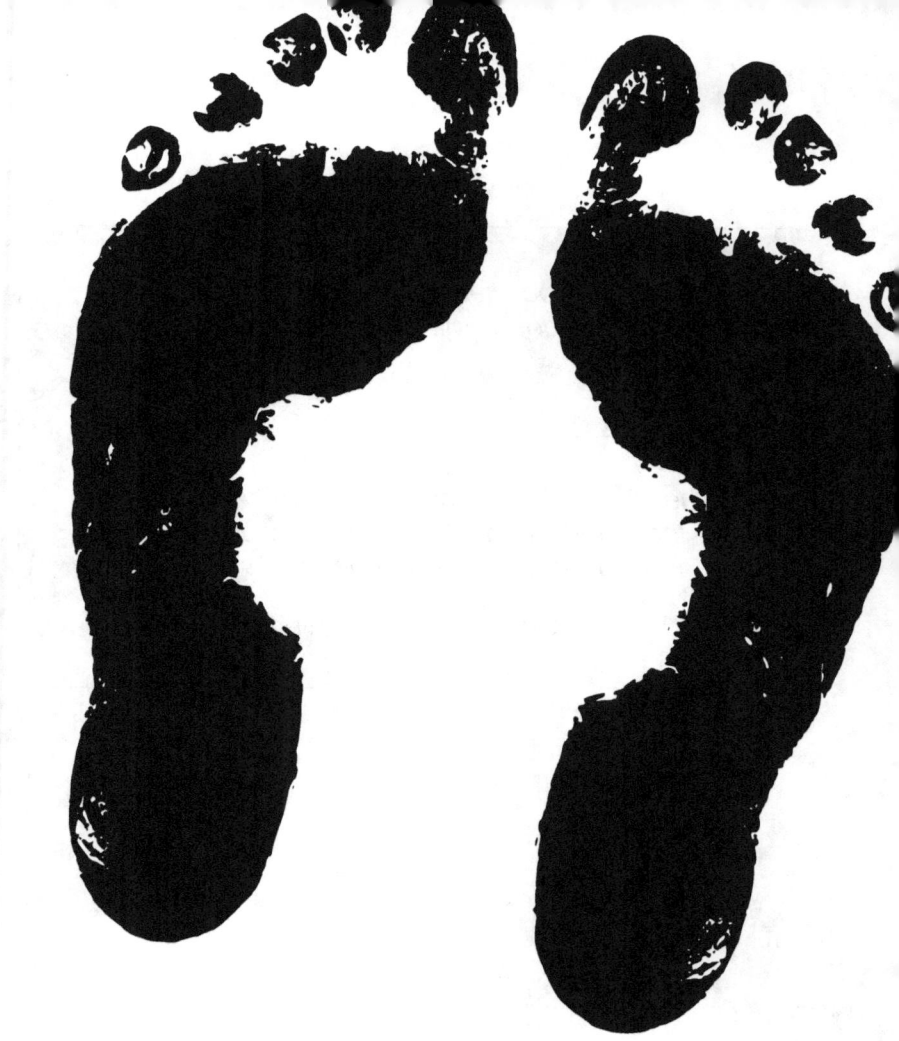

Step Twelve
Surrender

> "For you died, and your life is now hidden with Christ in God."
>
> —Colossians 3:3
>
> ---
>
> "The problem with making commitments to God is that their focus and success is based on us, and our effort...what we need is surrender."
>
> —Blackaby Ministries International

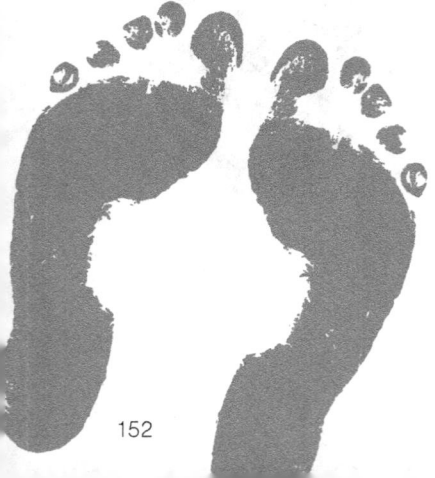

Step Twelve
Surrender

When I first met Rick, he was near the end of his life, for the first time. Rick had a brain tumor that had weakened him to the point he could not speak or rise from the bed. I worked to make him better, but he steadily grew more debilitated. He reached the point he could not swallow, and his wife Jamie was faced with the decision whether to place a feeding tube to prolong his life. All that we did for Rick eventually failed; finally, he was lying in a hospital room, dying unaware with ragged breathing. I saw him on evening rounds and handed him off to God, not expecting to see him again this side of heaven. The next morning, I checked on him, expecting him to be gone, and he was awake. Rick gradually improved and returned to full thinking, walking and testifying to God's mercy and power for one full year before his illness progressed and took him to heaven. I spoke with Jamie about this miracle, and she described to me the part she played in achieving it, "Through Rick's horrible illness, I prayed in tears that God would save him, that God would give you doctors wisdom, that God would not let my husband die. 'Do not take my Rick away from me!' And then came the day near the end, when all seemed lost. I gave up praying that God would save Rick. I lay face down on the floor with my hands spread out before the Lord and cried, 'He is yours, God. I give him up to you. Do what is best in your will.' The next day, Rick began to improve." Jamie had surrendered.

Eventually, in our decision-making, whatever the question, we need to get to the place Jamie found herself. We need to get to the place where we can fall on our faces and cry out, "It's yours, Lord. I give it up to you. Do what is best in your will." Eventually, and the sooner the better, we need to get to *surrender*.

In Step One, we spoke about the importance of *wanting God's will*. Surrender is the action that follows that desire. Surrender is intentionally handing off our circumstance, our decision, our life to God's will, whatever the outcome.

Each of the decision-making steps in this book eventually leads to surrender. Surrender is not giving up on our dreams; it is taking hold of God's dream instead. Surrender is not forsaking our heart's desire but taking for ourselves the heart of God. Surrender is not losing what we most want but gaining far more than we could have imagined.

At the end of my morning prayers each day, I finish with, "Dear Father, I surrender: all I am, all I have, all my dreams, all my plans, all those I love." I am quite sincere in my handing it all to Him, but I find myself taking much of it back for myself by the end of each day.

Blaise Paschal understood surrender. A brilliant man, who suffered physically much of his life, offered his own prayer of surrender to God. We quoted it with the first step in decision-making and it would be well to quote it again:

"I do not ask for health or sickness or life or death: I ask that you dispose of my health and sickness, my life and death—for your glory, for my salvation, for the use of your church and the saints of which I am a part...Give to me; take away from me; but make my will conform to yours."

Wanting God's will is the first step in decision-making. Letting go of our own, *surrender*, is the final step.

Surrender means being "all in" for Jesus.

> *One of my patients recently shared with me an event in his son's life that well describes being all in. Matt was having a great "date night" with his wife, away from the kids. She had just described a funny incident at home and Matt began laughing, but there must have been a bit of breadcrumb or meat*

in his throat and his laughter led to a severe coughing fit. His wife watched him turn red, sit straight up and fall backward to the tile restaurant floor, cracking open a starburst wound in the back of his head and bleeding profusely over the high-priced tile. His wife stood up screaming, and people ran over and gaped at the mess that was her husband. A restrained crowd gathered. Then one lady, finely dressed, stepped out of the gaping crowd, used her hand to close the wound and put pressure on the source of bleeding. Matt's blood covered the fine dress she had chosen specially for her night out with friends. My patient ended his story by declaring, "Lots of people were standing around, wanting Matt to get better, but that lady was all in."

"All in" is a life defined by devotion and obedience.

"All in" is a life of surrender.

"Since, then, you have been raised with Christ, set your hearts on things above, where Christ is seated at the right hand of God...For you died, and your life is now hidden with Christ in God" (Colossians 3:1-3).

We need to ask ourselves these "all in" questions.

Am I all in?

Do I love Jesus? Am I communicating with Him throughout my day?

Do I intentionally seek His goals for my life and service rather than my own?

Am I where He wants me to be, doing what He wants me to do?

Does my life reflect His sacrifice in active love for others?

Am I continually being delivered more and more from my sinful nature?

Am I speaking His name to those who do not know Him?

Do I really trust Him with the things I hold most dear?

> *Dr. David Stevens once provided a great example of surrender when we were fundraising to build the national headquarters for Christian Medical & Dental Associations: "Jody and I had decided what we could reasonably afford for the campaign and pledged that amount. It hurt a little financially, but we felt good about it. God then spoke to us and we decided to give a bit more. It was enough that it hurt more to give that amount, but we committed. God spoke again, and we pledged more; but it hurt more. And then God spoke again. We decided it was His will to give a large amount, an amount we could not really afford, larger than we had ever given to His service. We accepted His leadership and pledged that amount—and it began to feel good again."*

As Dave's story describes, surrender often passes through pain but eventually leads to a joy we would never have experienced without handing things over to Jesus.

The rich young ruler had a decision to make in Mark 10:17-22. He had come to Jesus with a great desire in his heart. "What must I do to inherit eternal life?" He pretty much had everything else. Besides that, he had been good, very good. Jesus checked him out with the Ten Commandments and he passed with flying colors. "All these I have kept since I was a boy."

"Jesus looked at him and loved him. 'One thing you lack,' he said. 'Go, sell everything you have and give to the poor, and you will have treasure in heaven. Then come, follow me.' At this, the man's face fell. He went away sad, because he had great wealth."

Why did this man miss the boat? Was it because he needed to have nothing so that he could follow Jesus? Do we need to give away all that we love to follow Jesus? Does surrender mean we come to Jesus owning nothing?

I don't believe that's the point of the encounter. The foundation of surrender is not that we come to Jesus with nothing. The foundation of surrender is that we come to Jesus with everything and offer it to Him for His use. The rich young ruler missed the boat, not because he was too rich, but because his wealth was the one thing he would not give to Jesus.

If we can sing, we don't give up singing in surrender to Jesus; we sing our hearts out wherever Jesus sends us. If we can run, we don't give up running until Jesus tells us to. If we have money, we don't have to give it all away before we can follow Jesus; we give it all to Jesus for His use and do what He tells us to do with our possessions.

Sometimes this may mean giving it all to the poor, as did Borden of Yale. Sometimes this means developing a foundation and handing it bit by bit to causes worthy of Jesus' name. Sometimes that may mean owning a lake house, used for His glory. But it always means, "This is yours, Lord. Use it as you will."

Surrender is taking our hands off the controls of our lives and off all we have. Surrender is that Carrie Underwood song, "Jesus, Take the Wheel." Surrender is saying, "I will follow you, Lord, whatever it takes" ...and that means with whatever decision lies before me.

When we surrender to God's will, that which matters most, we may lose for ourselves that which matters most. But, in His hands, our hearts will be transformed to accept a blessing from Him that matters far beyond our lost desire.

A few years after we returned from Nigeria, I had still not given up on the possibility of returning. I remember the day that dream died. It was a day of painful clarity for me. I would never serve my Lord in that way again. I put on my running shoes and ran with tears for miles. Totally spent, I gave to God what He required, the direction of my life. And He has made a wonder of it. I have lived an adventure with Christ that I would never have known had I held on to my dream of my best life for Him.

The basis of the Christian life is surrender—continually, repeatedly, setting aside our will and seeking God's will. Our initial step is to seek God's will. Our final step is setting aside our own to follow His.

Dag Hammarskjöld was the Secretary General of the United Nations when he died in a plane crash while trying to broker a peace treaty in Africa. He was a man of faith who saw himself as a stone in the slingshot of God. In his personal writings, *Markings*, as he moved forward into greater responsibility within the U.N., he wrote, "Long ago you gripped me, Slinger; now into the storm, now toward Your target!"

As Mr. Hammarskjöld suggested, we are not the Slinger; we are the stones. We need to settle into the sling and let God throw us where He will. Over and over, through the rest of our lives, we must ask ourselves the question, "Who gets to lead?"

Years ago, when I lived and worked in Nigeria, my local pastor and I spent one afternoon walking through the nearby village of Sanubi, visiting the few Christians there. Halfway through our visitation, we entered the concrete block, dirt floor home of an elderly Christian woman who was nearly blind. Her home was sparse, with a cot, a corner table, a plastic chair and little else.

When my pastor introduced us, she bobbed her head with a grin of pure joy. After she touched me, to be certain I was seated, she took a small plate, dusted it off, reached up under the tablecloth and pulled out a small coin. The coin was a kobo, worth less than a widow's mite, but valuable to her. She placed the kobo on a plate and held it out to me as a gift for our visit.

And so it goes with surrender. Compared to the God of the Universe, we are all as blind and poor as this Sanubi widow. Whatever our decision, we need with pure joy to place it before our King to use as He knows best. He knows; He cares; He can.

Next Steps

List the areas of your life over which you are still trying to keep control. Hand them over each day to Jesus.

_____

_____

_____

_____

_____

_____

_____

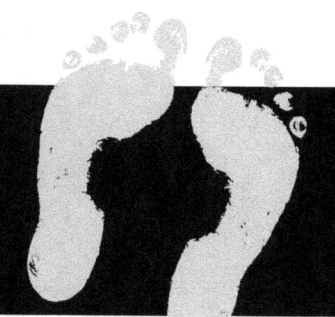

Dear Father,
I surrender: all I am, all I have, all my dreams, all my plans, all those I love.
Amen

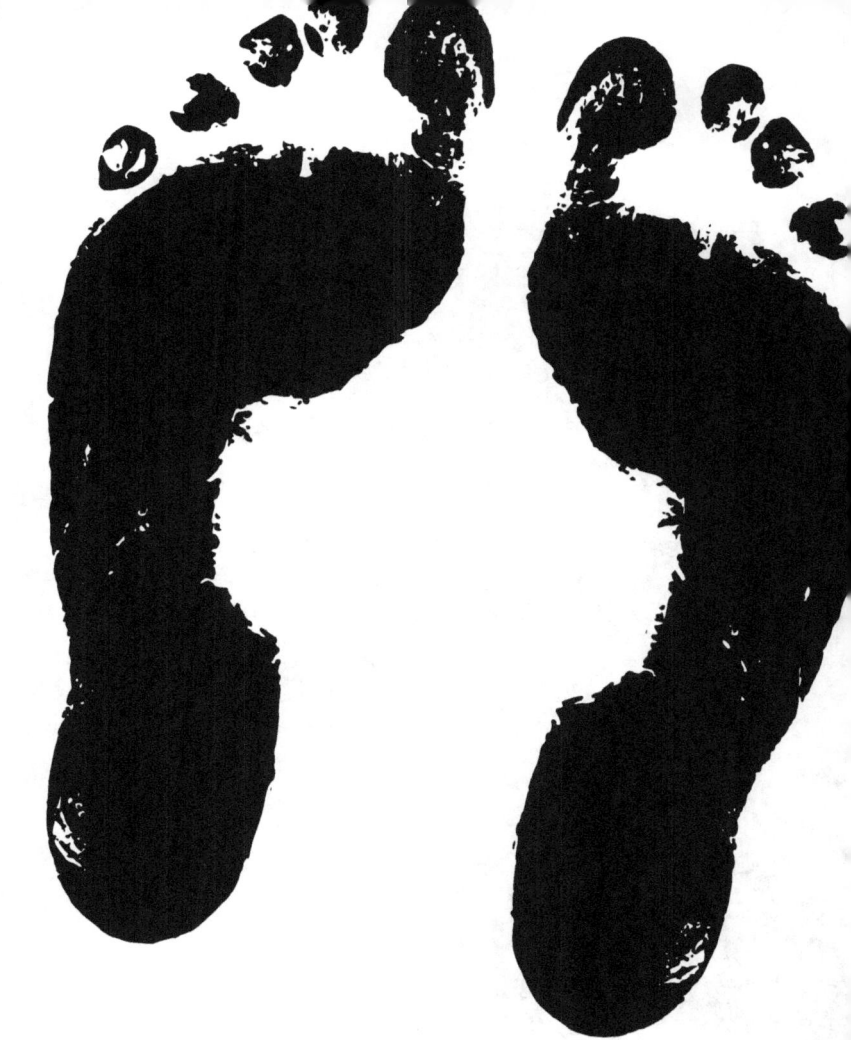

Critical Caveats

> *"These were all commended for their faith, yet none of them received what had been promised. God had planned something better for us...."*
>
> —Hebrews 11:39-40
>
> ---
>
> *"Leave everything to Him and it will be gloriously and graciously uncertain how He will come in—but you can be certain that He will come."*
>
> —Oswald Chambers

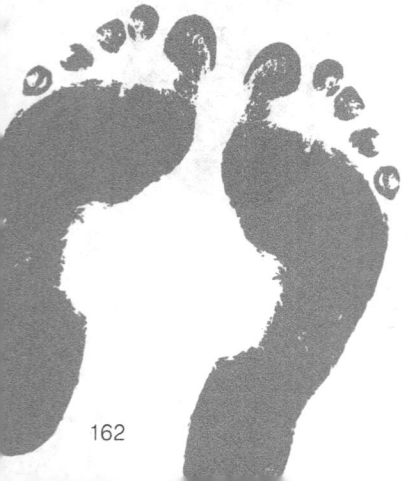

Critical Caveats

Twelve steps to landing in the middle of God's plan with your decision—guaranteed.

I am totally convinced by Scripture and by life experience that this is true. These twelve are not independent of each other but work together like the long line of determined people passing buckets from the beach to the burning town in Belize that I witnessed a few summers ago. Just as each person was important in that line, each step in decision-making is important and integrated with the others. Total disregard of any may break the chain and prevent our landing in God's will. Total commitment to each will absolutely place us on God's best path.

As with any system, other factors in life may confuse us as we place our feet on these twelve steps. We should mention them here.

It's Not the Need

One concern that drags many to places God would not choose is the cry of need from so many in this world. We must be clear that the need is not the call. There is more need in any place we put our feet than we can ever alleviate. In fact, when I was first headed to Nigeria, a neurosurgeon who consulted with me often on his cases said to me, "There is just as much need here in this city as there is in Africa." And he was right. There were more lost in Memphis and more deprived in my hometown than I could ever hope to satisfy.

Oswald Chambers was correct when he wrote, "Our Lord's first obedience was not to the needs of men, not to the consideration of where he was most useful, but to the will of His Father, and the first need of our life is not to be useful to God, but to do God's will."

It is certainly right to hold up the needs that grip our hearts to God and ask Him if He would let us work in those arenas, but God has a plan that encompasses the needs of all creation, and we must not be dragged away from His will by our hearts.

Clarity is Not Critical

So many of us are convinced that following God's will in a decision we need to make requires us to see God's plan clearly. This is just not so. Much of life, we will land on God's will without His explaining to us how we get there.

Philosopher John Cavanaugh visited Mother Teresa's Home for the Dying for three months in the 1970s. It was a time in his life when he was seeking direction from God for his own future. He was given the opportunity to have an audience with Teresa and asked her to pray for him.

"What would you have me pray?" she asked.

"Would you pray that God would give me clarity?" he said.

"I can't do that," she replied.

"Why not?" John asked.

"I have never had a day of clarity in my life," she said. "What I will pray for you is that you will learn to trust."

Clarity or trust?

My 2-year-old granddaughter loves to play in my study, but if the lights are off, she will stop before she enters and say, "Turn lights on, Doc."

When we were children, many of us were afraid of the dark. Some of us still are. As human beings, we want to know where we are going before we decide where God wants us to work for the next 10 years, or whether we should marry, or how to give financially, or whom to trust with the health of our sick child. The world in which we humans exist has been broken down into data and probability factors. We evaluate what we can see, make the best judgment based on observation and then choose how to act. We know emergency surgery on a traumatic belly is far more anxiety provoking than a planned-ahead cholecystectomy. We prefer to know what we will find before we explore.

Unfortunately, this way of thinking is not always accurate when it carries over into our faith life. It is difficult for me to decide on a direction in my life when I am not sure where it will take me. If I can't see the future clearly, I become frustrated and anxious over my next step. Even though I see a bit of God's will and trust Him to carry it out, I still can't get over my fear of the dark.

When I read God's Word, I see Him saying over and over again, "Your understanding of my will is not nearly as important as your wanting my will and your trusting in me as you step into the darkness." That's what Abraham's call to be a "wandering Aramean" was all about. His total trust was the very foundation upon which God has led His people through the centuries—even to the foot of the cross, even to my next decision.

Trust is critical. Clarity is not.

Peace is Not Guaranteed

Some of us are convinced that we can perceive God's best choice because we feel His peace rest upon us with the reassurance of a loving Father. And often, God will provide this peace for us as a sign we are going in the right direction—but not always. There have been times in my life where I knew I was in the center of God's plan with a decision and yet was troubled immensely, especially as the journey began. In fact, one of the ways we might gain a hint that we are on God's path is the fear or frustration that often assails us once we begin to follow our understanding of His will.

> *Mother Teresa lived a life certain of God's presence, but very often lived without the peace of presence one would expect from so dedicated a servant of Christ. She would often speak of it to her spiritual supervisors. On one occasion, after receiv-*

ing 13 new postulants to help her in her work, she wrote the following letter to Father Neuner: "We got 13 new postulants last Jan. and they already seem full of the joy of suffering for God's poor...Since God wants me to abstain from the joy of the riches of spiritual life—I am giving my whole heart and soul to helping my Sisters to make full use of it. I see them grow day by day in holiness—see them grow in the love of God—and the seeing makes me happy. As for myself, I just have the joy of having nothing—not even the reality of the Presence of God. No prayer, no love, no faith—nothing but continual pain of longing for God." (from Mother Teresa: Come Be My Light*)*

Being in the center of God's will and knowing you are there does not guarantee we will feel great peace.

When God first called my wife and me to Africa, there were the times of extreme lack of peace I described earlier. Even in retrospect, after a shortened international experience, I have no doubt we were in the center of God's will with our decision to serve Him in Nigeria.

"Conflict often comes with our choosing God's path." This truth has become so clear to me that I frequently warn those who are passionately following Christ with a decision in their lives. I warn them that they are about to face a time of real struggle, and that warning usually comes true. I do not know whether this is God building character and faith, or if it is Satan opposing God's plan; nevertheless, the difficulties do come and the peace that we had imagined should follow our obedience often wanders off. Eventually that peace does return with a knowledge of God's presence that is much stronger than before; it becomes a peace that "passes all understanding," forged out of walking with God through the valley of anxiety and fear, finding that He has been there with us and His love is able to overcome all that has threatened us. Peace will come as He promised but not always at the point of a final decision.

Presently, my wife and I are trying to simplify our lives by selling off many of our assets so we might be free to follow God's direction more faithfully. There is nothing peaceful about selling off our assets. It requires letting go of things we cherish, dealing with irritating people, questioning the outcome at the other side of simplification. I have no peace in the process, but I do have a confidence in this decision that comes from seeking God's will and finding it.

Our God is a God whose very presence brings peace, but we must never use personal peace as a reliable measuring stick to accept or deny the direction that God might carry us.

The Time Factor

Very often we are forced to make decisions before we feel we have had enough time to work through the decision-making process. We come to the day we have to decide, and God has not given us His clear word. "It's now, God! What do you want me to do?" And God just seems to sit back with His arms crossed in silence. Things are moving too fast and God has just not kept up with the process.

In an earlier chapter I shared the story of my ophthalmologist friend who had to rush through an impossible day. At the end of that day, he discovered that no matter what the time pressure, God can keep up. He could for my friend, and He can for you.

Sometimes we move so fast through life out of necessity that we feel like we have left God's Spirit behind. We come to a point of decision and feel we are alone without His presence or final word. We want God's will but have no more time to seek it. My friend would tell you after his day, "Go ahead and make your decision with what you have. You are not making it alone. God has not been left behind. No matter what your urgency, God can keep up."

The Problem of Fear

Sometimes when we settle into God's path, the fear we find may dare us to turn back or to question the decision we made that has placed us here. Just as peace is not an absolute measuring stick to convince us we have made the right decision, fear is not an absolute measuring stick to tell us we have turned the wrong way.

The disciples gathered around Jesus were convinced He was the one to follow. His most trusted disciples waited for Him as He prayed in the Garden of Gethsemane. But then came Judas into the garden with his kiss of betrayal, and they suddenly questioned whether they had made the right decision to follow this charismatic teacher. In their fear, they all ran away, except for Peter who followed long enough to deny the Christ because of his fear. Fear can make us refuse to take the path our God would ask us to follow, and fear may cause us to step off that path once we began the journey. How does one overcome fear that might set us on the wrong path when we are seeking a Godly decision?

The best antidote for the poison of fear is "presence."

> *Barbara was a patient of mine with breast cancer. I sat across from her in my examining room and discussed her widespread disease. She was 75 years old and knew she would not live much longer. "When I was a young girl, I remember a huge slide in my backyard, or at least it was huge to me. I remember sitting at the top of that slide afraid to let go, but I finally did. You see, my daddy was at the bottom of the slide calling to me, 'You can let go. I am here to catch you.' I did, and he did. That's how I am moving ahead with this cancer and what it brings. God is like my daddy at the bottom of the slide. I've lived long enough and slid down enough slides to know He is there to catch me."*

I had a similar experience when I was a young boy. When I was a child, my greatest time of uncertainty was Christmas morning. My parents compounded our anxious anticipation by making us stand at the top of the stairs while my father prepared all the complicated home movie lights. Only after the set up was complete were we able to walk slowly down the stairs toward our Christmas, waving politely into the blinding movie lights. For us as children, all the important stuff of the morning was behind those blinding lights, underneath the Christmas tree.

We could never be certain at the top of the stairs that we would find under the tree what we had asked for and dreamed of. In spite of that, we were excited and confident rather than fearful and anxious. We were confident Christmas morning would bring us joy because we knew the man behind the lights, the man who had prepared our Christmas morning for us. Even when I did not find what I expected under the tree, what I did find was always wonderful.

Just so with life—I cannot see beyond the blinding lights or cold darkness that hide my future, but I do know Who is out there, calling me into my future. We may often be uncertain of events ahead of us in this life, but we can always be certain of the One who calls us forth. As Oswald Chambers put it in *My Utmost for His Highest*, "Leave everything to Him and it will be gloriously and graciously uncertain how He will come in—but you can be certain that He will come."

We must not fear uncertainty and we also must not fear certainty.

> *She was so young, late 30s with young children, facing the certain debilitation and death her brain tumor promised. She had traveled a few months down that road and was in my office for a follow-up exam. Limping in with weakness on the right side of her body, she pulled herself up onto the examining table as her mother followed her into the room. After her examination, she stepped down from the table but made the mistake of stepping onto her weak side. With her right leg unable to support her, she began to fall; however, her mother was quick and ready and grabbed her as she tottered, protecting her from the floor. She then stood straight and looked at me with the most beautiful smile I had ever seen and said, "You see; I've got my Momma on my right and Jesus on my left. I can't possibly fall."*

Twelve Steps

Our future lies before us. We cannot avoid taking a step. Each step demands a decision on our part. Which way? We can make those decisions in a utilitarian way, as those who do not know God: choosing the path most likely to produce the most pleasure and the least pain. Or we can make our decisions hand in hand with the One who holds our future and offers it back to us with the freedom of choice.

Twelve steps, all focused on finding God's best plan for us and best plan for all He has created, a plan totally grounded in His love for us, totally envisioned by His omniscience, totally backed by His power. The real question is, "Do we most want to be part of God's plan, or do we most want to be part of our own?" If we can but get this question right, so much else in decision-making is laid before us as we travel.

With each of our decisions, we should seek to get it right, seek to get it God's way. These twelve steps should get us very close. But even doing our best, we are still human and will fail at times. When we fail, we must remember that all is grace.

Grace

Grace is always the final point. The most beautiful thing about all our decision-making is that all is grace. If we are followers of Christ who long to do His will with most of our lives, the same cross in the heart of God that saves us from death is the cross that accepts our decisions, good or bad, and loves us through the consequences.

God's heroes in the Bible did not always make good decisions.

When Abraham was on his journey to God's unknown destination, he traveled with great faith; but, out of fear in Egypt, he made the decision to tell Pharaoh that his wife was his sister, landing her in the Pharaoh's harem. Yet God still holds Abraham up in Scripture as a great example of faith.

When Peter followed Jesus into the courtyard of the high priest, he made the decision to deny knowing Jesus; yet, Peter is still called the rock upon which the church is built.

We do our best in this world as followers of Jesus to follow Him in our decision-making. Taking the twelve steps in this book will likely place us on His perfect path with those decisions. We will do our best, and we will sometimes fail.

God's grace covers it all.

We may suffer the consequences of our unfaithful choices, but the cross stands as a reminder that we will never be separated from the One we failed.

Recently, the vocal artist Colton Dixon sang a song that has filled me with God's grace as I look back over a life where many of my decisions were just flat wrong. The chorus of Dixon's song goes like this:

"I have won; I have lost
I got it right sometimes and sometimes I did not
Life is a journey; I've seen joy; I've seen regret—
And You have been my God through all of it."

Amen.

Next Steps

Review each step below and place a check next to it when you are confident God has you where He wants you in this present decision. They are purposely out of order.

☐ Wanting God's Will
☐ Listen Hard
☐ Obedience
☐ Remove the Sin that Binds and Blinds
☐ Seek Wise Counsel
☐ Respect Your Passions
☐ Gather the Facts
☐ Surrender
☐ The Centrality of Abiding
☐ Follow His Word
☐ Trust
☐ Choose Your Target

www.ingramcontent.com/pod-product-compliance
Lightning Source LLC
Chambersburg PA
CBHW070602010526
44118CB00012B/1419